921
VIC

GRANT
Victori

25974

DATE DUE

MR 13 '91
OCT 2 1 1994
NOV 2 7 1996
JAN 1 1 1996
MAY 1 5 1998
JAN 0 9 2003

DISCARDED

NORTH HIGH MEDIA CENTER
1042 SCHOOL AVENUE
SHEBOYGAN, WI 53081

DEMCO

Victoria
Queen and Empress

Victoria, Queen of the United Kingdom of Great Britain and Ireland, and Empress of India. (Charles Phelps Cushing)

Immortals of History

Victoria
Queen and Empress

by Neil Grant

Franklin Watts, Inc.
575 Lexington Avenue
New York, N.Y. 10022

SBN 531-00959-9
Copyright © 1970 by Franklin Watts, Inc.
Library of Congress Catalog Card Number 73-121922
Manufactured in the United States of America

1 2 3 4 5 6 7 8

25974
NORTH HIGH SCHOOL LIBRARY
Sheboygan, Wisconsin

Contents

	Introduction	vii
I	The Lonely Princess	3
II	Lord Melbourne Explains	17
III	"He Is an Angel"	33
IV	A Happy Family	51
V	Trials and Triumphs of Prince Albert	63
VI	War and Alliances	73
VII	An End and a Beginning	85
VIII	Endurance	99
IX	"Wumman" and "Faery"	111
X	Liberalism	127
XI	The British Empire	143
XII	Empress of India	155
XIII	Tragedy in Khartoum	169
XIV	Golden Jubilee	185

CONTENTS

XV	Imperialism	197
XVI	End of an Age	211
	Chronology	223
	Note on Sources and Books	227
	Index	229

Introduction

Queen Victoria reigned longer than any other English monarch. She came to the throne of Great Britain as a girl of eighteen in 1837 and she died at the age of eighty-one in the second year of the twentieth century.

During those years, Great Britain reached the height of its power and prestige. Its railroads, factories, and banks grew faster than those of any other country. Its powerful navy defended an ever-expanding empire that reached to every continent. It was an age of rapid change and confident progress. In 1837 Britain was still a land of small towns and villages; by the end of the century the mass of the people lived in sprawling industrial cities. Modern states based on British traditions were established in North America and Australasia, and British institutions were re-created in the lands of the new British Empire in Asia and Africa. The old land-owning aristocracy of England retreated before the rising class of businessmen and bankers; and the prosperous middle classes, with their serious attitude toward life, their belief in the value of hard work and prayer, and their pride in their own institutions and beliefs, came to set the tone of society.

The views held by Queen Victoria often reflected the attitudes of her subjects. As her last prime minister said after her death: ". . . when I knew what the Queen thought, I knew pretty certainly what views her subjects would take, especially the middle class of her subjects." That was one reason for the immense respect and affection that Victoria commanded in the later years of her reign.

Victoria became a living legend, not only in England but throughout the British Empire. An African tribal chieftain, when told of her death, expected to see another star in the sky. A Tibetan tribe worshipped her as a goddess.

Nevertheless the power of the crown in government, which was not very clearly defined, actually diminished during Victoria's reign. But what it lost in direct power it gained in influence and prestige. In 1837 it was far from certain that monarchy would survive in Britain, but despite the strong tide of republicanism flowing throughout Europe, by 1901 the continued existence of the monarchy was assured.

INTRODUCTION

This was perhaps Queen Victoria's greatest personal achievement.

Queen Victoria's character—at once simple and complex—is a fascinating study. Although she lacked any outstanding intellectual gifts, no ordinary person could have gained such a remarkable success in public relations. But her fame rests not only on her own life and character. She was above all the national emblem of Britain and of the British Empire. Her long reign and great reputation made her the personification of her age—the most glorious age in English history since the reign of her predecessor Queen Elizabeth. More than a queen-empress, before her death she had become a powerful combination of sovereign, mother, and priestess.

Victoria
Queen and Empress

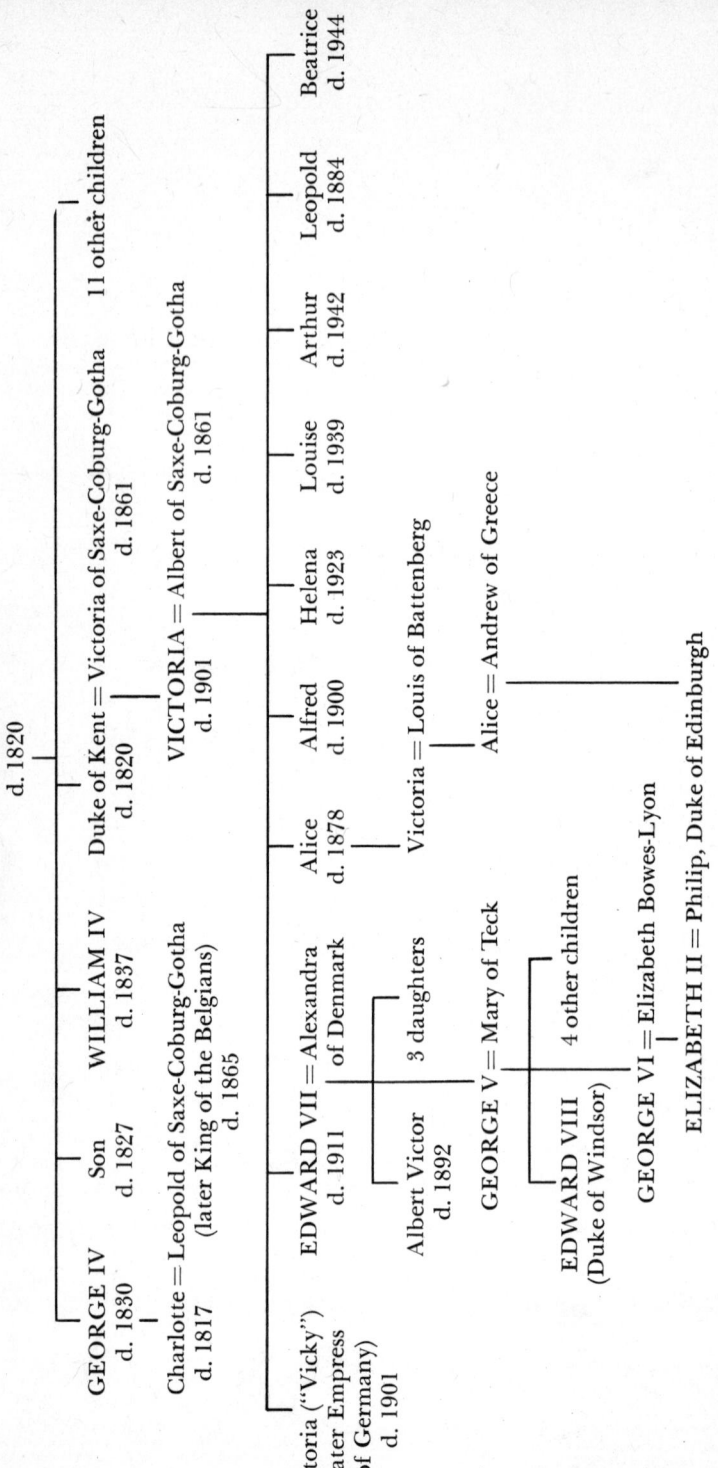

CHAPTER I

The Lonely Princess

King George III of England, who reigned from 1760 to 1820, had no less than fifteen children; but, as he sometimes grumbled, they were "a poor lot," his sons especially. The old king's subjects rated the royal princes no higher than he did, and the poet Percy Bysshe Shelley summed up the general feeling when he described them as "the dregs of their dull race."

One of the most annoying things about George III's sons was their dislike of the institution of marriage. Instead of settling down with a suitable princess for a wife, they preferred a less official partnership with their pleasant—but not royal mistresses. Since these princes made no marriages, they produced no legitimate children, and despite the size of George III's family, the royal line was in danger of extinction.

The heir to the throne (who was to become George IV) did have one brief and disastrous marriage which produced a solitary daughter, Princess Charlotte. When Charlotte married a German prince, everyone breathed a sigh of relief. Through her issue the royal line would be continued. But unhappily, Princess Charlotte died in giving birth to her first child. This child died with her, and the situation was worse than before.

At this point, Parliament took a hand. The royal dukes were drawing large pensions from the government, which allowed them to live in luxury with their mistresses. If they wanted their pensions to continue, declared Parliament, they must do their duty to their country. Let them put aside their mistresses, get married, and above all, produce some heirs!

The Duke of Kent, third son of George III, bowed reluctantly to Parliament's wishes. Sorrowfully discarding the French lady he had lived with for nearly thirty years, he proposed marriage to a widowed German princess of the house of Saxe-Coburg-Gotha (the same family as Princess Charlotte's husband). After some diplomatic hesitation, the princess agreed to become Duchess of Kent.

What was so obviously a marriage of convenience between the elderly English prince and the not-so-young German widow turned out surprisingly well. They were happy together, but they were not together very long. Less than two years after the wedding, the

THE LONELY PRINCESS

hearty, robust duke caught a cold. He did not take proper care of it and it turned into pneumonia. In a few days he was dead.

Besides the grieving duchess, the English duke left behind him a mass of debts and one small daughter, the princess Victoria, born on May 24, 1819.

Queen Victoria later said her childhood was unhappy. Her German mother was short of money and suspicious of her royal English relatives; they lived in isolation at Kensington Palace, near London, with a small court in attendance. Princess Victoria had no children of her own age to play with. As heir to the throne, her education was strict, and though she was intelligent, she was not studious by nature. True, Victoria was good at languages, and she liked history, but Latin and religious teachings came hard to her. Music was more to her taste, although piano practice was boring. But she did enjoy drawing. Her dancing teacher (who was a lady, for it was not considered "respectable" for the princess to learn dancing from a man) helped to develop her natural poise, for which she later became famous.

Deportment was very important for a future queen. Her mother would tie a sprig of prickly holly under Victoria's chin to make her hold her head up—a severe but effective measure.

The worst part of Victoria's education was not the lessons themselves but the long hours. The princess did not have much time to run about outside or play with the various pets she loved so much. She was constantly supervised. Every night of her life, until she became queen, Victoria slept in her mother's bedroom. Her governess, and often her mother too, sat in the schoolroom during her lessons, and the little girl was not allowed to go downstairs without someone holding her hand in case she slipped.

Victoria came to know that she was of high birth because gentlemen raised their hats to her—but not to other little girls. When she was eleven years old, she opened her history book one day to find that someone had stuck in a new page. It was a family tree of English royalty. She stared at it for a moment—then the truth dawned. *She* was heir to the throne! She looked up at her smiling teacher and raised her right hand. "I will be good," she said solemnly, and burst into tears.

As Victoria grew older, she became uncomfortably aware that she was the center of political intrigues and family feuds. The man chiefly responsible for the unpleasant and suspicious atmosphere that surrounded the princess was her mother's steward, Sir John Conroy. In the story of Queen Victoria's childhood, this disreputable man is the villain of the piece. Conroy had plenty of charm when he cared to use it, but behind it was concealed an insatiable greed for money and power. He completely conquered the duchess, and people supposed he was her lover.

Secretly, he helped himself to the duchess's cash, although this was not discovered until years later.

Victoria stood next in line to the throne after her uncles George IV and William IV. Conroy expected both those gentlemen to die before Victoria was old enough to reign. The duchess would then be regent, and Conroy himself would be the power behind the throne—or so he planned. His evil influence hung like a black cloud over Kensington Palace, and as the princess came to understand his schemes she learned to hate him and to despise her mother who was so thoroughly in his power.

Yet Victoria had allies of her own at Kensington. The most important was Baroness Lehzen, her companion, guide, and friend. Narrow-minded and too fond of gossip, this long-nosed German woman had one supreme virtue—loyalty. She was put in charge of Victoria when the princess was five, and for the next eighteen years she hardly ever left her side. She supervised Victoria's waking hours and sat in the bedroom until the duchess came to bed. Though strict, she devoted herself entirely to Victoria, battling fiercely against Conroy and acting as a substitute mother when her charge turned against the duchess. In return for this selfless service, Victoria lavished all her affection on Lehzen, calling her "the most estimable & precious treasure I possess."

Lehzen's influence was restricted to the household

at Kensington, but the princess had at least one ally in the great political world—her uncle Leopold (whose first wife was Princess Charlotte). Leopold became king of the Belgians in 1830, and after that he was not often at Kensington, but his long letters helped to compensate for his absence. Cool-headed and ambitious, King Leopold was one of the ablest statesmen of his time. He exerted a powerful influence on the fatherless princess by his good sense and tact—qualities quite lacking in her mother and Sir John Conroy. Leopold hoped she would one day marry his nephew, Albert of Saxe-Coburg-Gotha, who had been born in Germany in the same year as Victoria. Because he treated Victoria as a sensible person and not a property to be controlled or bargained for, Leopold deserved—and achieved—better success with her than did the self-seeking Conroy.

The atmosphere of intrigue and the hatreds it provoked might well have had a disastrous effect on a young girl. Fortunately, the princess displayed from early childhood a toughness of character that was to see her through many crises in her long life.

Other characteristics of the mature woman were also present in the child. For example, her honesty—she was incapable of telling a lie even to save herself from punishment. When it was not safe to speak, she learned to keep silent.

Not surprisingly, the princess occasionally showed a streak of ruthless selfishness. From the cradle she was the center of attention, and with so many different influences tugging at her, her determination to have her own way if possible was a natural and necessary reaction. She was not a rebel by nature, though subject to fits of rage, or "storms," as she called them.

While she was never beautiful, the young Victoria made a pretty figure at court or in the gardens at Kensington. She was small and slim, with large blue eyes and fair hair. Her nose, if not quite hooked, was definitely curved, and it hinted at the strength of character that was not apparent in her small, receding chin.

The pressures of life at Kensington did not suppress her hearty laugh—head thrown back, mouth wide open—which critical courtiers thought was ungraceful. Perhaps her most attractive feature—present throughout her life—was her silvery voice. Many people noticed how beautifully she pronounced the English language, perhaps because it was not, strictly speaking, her native tongue. The first words she learned were German.

When King William IV came to the throne in 1830, he announced that he expected to see more of his niece and heir at court. The duchess and Conroy resented this demand, afraid of losing their influence over Victoria. The little princess was not even allowed to attend her Uncle William's coronation, although she watched the procession, in tears, from a window.

Two years later, Conroy organized a series of tours

Victoria as she appeared during her girlhood. (Charles Phelps Cushing)

THE LONELY PRINCESS

around England for the heir to the throne. It seemed a good idea, for the future queen saw something of the country, and the country saw something of her. The chief purpose of the tours, however, was to gain popularity for Victoria (and for the duchess and Conroy) at the expense of King William, who was furious at the idea of his heir progressing around the kingdom receiving the cheers of *his* subjects. Wherever she went, guns fired a royal salute. Stop that "popping," the angry king commanded. But Conroy smiled his roguish smile and the "popping" continued.

On these tours, which sometimes lasted as long as three months, Lehzen persuaded the princess to keep a diary. With her vivid style, decisive opinions, and sense of duty, Victoria turned out to be a very good diarist. For the rest of her life, hardly a day went by without some comment in Victoria's journal. Thanks to this stern self-discipline, historians have a detailed record of Victoria's life, from childhood to the grave.

In 1835, the princess's battle with Conroy heated up as relations between Kensington and the king's court grew worse. There was trouble at Victoria's confirmation when the crusty old king ordered Conroy out of the chapel. Then, ignoring Victoria's protests, Conroy organized a grand tour of northern England, with renewed "popping" to irritate the king.

A visit from Leopold, the *"dearest* of Uncles, who has always been to me like a father," brightened the fall. For hours he talked to his niece about the duties of a sovereign. Do not trust anyone unless you are sure of him, he warned, and never answer a question until you have thought it over. The princess absorbed it all.

Soon after her uncle had gone, Victoria was stricken with a dangerous attack of fever. She was seriously ill for a month and did not fully recover until the spring of the following year. Sir John Conroy took advantage of her weakened state to try to mold her to his will.

Victoria might soon be queen, he told her. She would need a private secretary. What better choice for the post than himself? Pale and exhausted as she was, the princess shook her head. Sir John urged his case more strongly. All she had to do was to sign a piece of paper—he had it with him, and a pen to sign it. The princess said no. Lehzen stood by her, hissing and snapping at Sir John, who fiercely denounced her for her loyalty to Victoria. The princess still resisted, and at last Sir John retired, defeated.

This was not the end of the matter, Conroy still hoped that the king would die before Victoria's eighteenth birthday. If he did, the Duchess of Kent would be regent, and Conroy's position would be secure.

The king, who loathed Conroy and the duchess, meant to thwart them both, if possible, by living long enough for Victoria to succeed him without a regent. When the duchess and her daughter attended his seventy-first birthday dinner, he made a speech attacking the Kensington Palace regime. He protested angrily that Victoria had been kept away from court, and he expressed the hope that the duchess, surrounded as she was by "evil advisers" (he meant Conroy), would never be regent of England. It was a highly embarrassing incident, and once again poor Victoria was reduced to tears.

Later, King William tried to get Victoria away from the duchess by offering the princess a court of her own with a large income to maintain it. This would have ruined Conroy's plans. The duchess and her steward forced the princess to sign a letter rejecting the offer. The king was not deceived. "Victoria has not written that," he said when he read it.

By now Victoria and her mother were not on speaking terms. When the duchess had something to say to her daughter, she sent a note via a messenger. But life was not all conflict for Victoria. Visits from her foreign relatives delighted the princess, and in May, 1836, on the eve of her seventeenth birthday, she waited with nervous excitement to greet her cousins Albert of Saxe-Coburg-Gotha and his elder brother Ernest. This visit was engineered by King Leopold, who planned a marriage between his German nephew Albert and his English niece. King William, who disliked the idea, was tempted to bar the German princes from the country, but the prime minister persuaded him that such conduct would be regarded as tyranny.

The young men arrived, and the princess, just three

months older than Albert, was delighted with them both. Albert, she thought, was "extremely handsome," and two weeks of his company made her even more enthusiastic. "He possesses every quality that could be desired to render me perfectly happy," she told her uncle Leopold. That ambitious monarch might well feel pleased with himself, but he wisely refrained from pushing the young couple any closer together at that stage.

On May 24, 1837, Victoria celebrated her eighteenth birthday. It was not a joyous occasion. Sir John Conroy watched her through the whole evening, and she felt thoroughly nervous. The duchess and her steward had not given up hope of persuading Victoria to ask for a regency, though since she was eighteen, it was not constitutionally necessary.

King William IV had accomplished his object of living until Victoria was old enough to reign, but having done so, he faded rapidly away. Less than a month later, it was obvious he was dying. Conroy made desperate efforts to force Victoria's agreement to his plans; he spoke of locking her up until she consented, but the duchess would not agree to such barbaric behavior. The princess kept to her room anyway, and talked to no one but Lehzen.

In the early hours of June 20, King William died. At once the archbishop of Canterbury and the lord chamberlain rode through the night to Kensington. It was still dark when they arrived, and the porter refused to let them in. After an argument, Baroness Lehzen was notified, and she came fluttering downstairs, her long nose twitching in excitement. She roused the duchess, and together they woke Victoria. The archbishop and the lord chamberlain waited impatiently downstairs.

At last the door opened and a small figure in a cotton bathrobe, fair hair streaming down onto her shoulders, entered the room—alone. The lord chamberlain knelt to kiss the hand of the Queen of England.

CHAPTER II

Lord Melbourne Explains

The popularity of the monarchy in Great Britain had fallen very low when Queen Victoria came to the throne. For more than a century, the English people had not had a monarch they could wholeheartedly admire. George I, a German, spoke almost no English; George II was little better; George III made too many mistakes; George IV was a playboy; and finally, William IV looked and sounded more like a sea captain than a king. During her long reign, Queen Victoria was to raise the prestige of the crown to heights it had never reached before.

She started off with several things in her favor. After her fat old uncles, she herself was a pleasant change. A young, innocent girl with large blue eyes and a ready smile naturally attracted sympathy. People felt protective toward her. When the historian Thomas Carlyle saw her go by in her carriage, he felt "heartily sorry for the poor [child]." Yet Victoria was not quite as innocent and helpless as she looked. The long battle with Conroy and her own determined character equipped her well for the ordeals ahead.

The ministers and officials who attended Victoria on the first morning of her reign were amazed at her coolness. She entered the council chamber alone and, except that her cheeks were slightly flushed, showed not a sign of emotion. The royal dukes knelt to her, the great men of the kingdom kissed her hand. In her clear, steady voice she read a short speech, then, still alone, she withdrew.

A hum of enthusiastic comment broke out as the door closed behind her. What grace, what poise, what a beautiful voice, what regal dignity!

In another room, Victoria found her mother waiting. Politely she asked the duchess to leave her alone for an hour. This first request of the young queen brought a sudden chill to her mother's heart, and she was not reassured when she found out that her bed had been moved out of Victoria's room—at the queen's order.

Others were soon to find that this innocent girl was no helpless puppet. She must, she was told, ride in a carriage to take the salute at the Hyde Park Review. To ride on horseback without any female companions might be considered indelicate. "What nonsense!" declared the queen. Her ministers insisted. "A horse or nothing," she replied. Regretfully, her ministers decided it would have to be nothing, and the Hyde Park Review was canceled.

Attendance at such ceremonies as the Hyde Park Review was one side of the queen's royal duties. But what was the real function of the crown when Victoria ascended the throne? What powers and obligations did she have as sovereign?

Walter Bagehot, whose famous book on the British constitution was published in 1867, wrote that the rights of the sovereign in government were: to be consulted, to give encouragement, and to issue warnings. Queen Victoria would not have agreed with this view. She would have claimed the right to oppose a government whose policy she disapproved of, and even perhaps to dismiss a prime minister she did not like. She felt that her warnings ought to be heeded and her advice acted on.

Undoubtedly Victoria exaggerated her powers, but as they were nowhere precisely defined, some difference of opinion was possible. While Victoria strictly adhered in theory to her slightly exalted view of her powers, she never pushed them too hard in practice. Thus she would later dislike William Gladstone and loath his policies, but she never considered trying to dismiss him as prime minister. She had too much common sense to risk causing a constitutional crisis over the powers of the crown, which might well have ended in a full-scale revolution against the monarchy.

In fact, while the prestige of the crown expanded enormously during Victoria's reign, its actual power declined. These two facts are connected: If Victoria had tried to play the same kind of active political role as her grandfather, George III, the crown would have become involved in petty political feuds and party strife. It was only by avoiding sordid controversies of that sort that the prestige of the monarchy could be raised.

While Queen Victoria soon showed that she had a mind of her own, she knew almost nothing about the ways of the world. Life in Kensington Palace was not very much different from life in a nunnery. This unworldly and inexperienced teen-ager, suddenly transferred to the throne of England, needed help and advice. Of course there was Lehzen, nibbling away happily at the caraway seeds she was so fond of, and privately celebrating the banishment of the duchess and her steward to a remote wing of Buckingham Palace. There was Uncle Leopold, offering advice and encouragement in his long and sensible letters. And, better still, there was Leopold's agent and friend, Baron Stockmar, a skillful, self-effacing German doctor who flitted through the political salons of Europe and carried in his head all kinds of good ideas for the guidance of a young queen.

Unfortunately, these friends and helpers shared one serious drawback. They were all foreigners.

Victoria really needed a private secretary closely connected with English politics. It was not easy to find a suitable man. Lord Melbourne, the prime minister and leader of the Whig party, considered several candidates and finally decided to take the job on himself. So began a fascinating relationship.

When Queen Victoria ascended the throne, the Whig prime minister was fifty-eight, forty years her senior. A fine example of the aristocratic ruling class, he was still a handsome man, with large dark eyes and long lashes. His political career had been calm, unexciting, and very successful. He had entered politics because that was what men in his station of life usually did, not out of ambition for power. Lord Melbourne had no ambition, nor did he need any. Every success seemed to fall into his hands without his seeking it and apparently without his wanting it. When told he was to be prime minister, his answer was, "I think it's a damned bore."

Although he was the leader of the Whigs, the party of change, Melbourne was by nature a conservative, with a rather cynical view of human affairs. Reform of Parliament would not do any good, he said. Of what use was the vote? Or education? Or any sort of progress? Still, his pessimism was graced by humor. He was renowned as one of the best talkers in Europe, and examples of his wit pepper the pages of Victoria's journal. His lounging about and rough language (carefully moderated in the queen's presence) dis-

A portrait of Lord Melbourne. (National Portrait Gallery)

guised keen sensitivity and intelligence. While it was true, alas, that he sometimes went to sleep at cabinet meetings, it was also true that for amusement in the evenings he used to read the New Testament in Greek.

The public success which came so easily to Lord Melbourne had not been paralleled in his private life. His stormy marriage to a beautiful but hopelessly unstable woman ended in tragedy, and largely explained his cynicism. The only product of the marriage was a retarded son who died shortly before Victoria's accession.

In the young queen, Melbourne found a person he could devote himself to, as, in the early years of his marriage, he had devoted himself to his wife. His fatherly feelings too were drawn forth by the innocence and exuberance of Victoria. With neither wife nor children to care for, Lord Melbourne poured forth all the love of his affectionate nature on the queen.

King Leopold had told the queen to trust the prime minister as her friend, and she found their first conversation "very *comfortable*." Her opinion soon became more enthusiastic as Melbourne's charm cast its spell. All her young life Victoria had been looking for a father to replace the one she had lost as an infant. Leopold had come nearest to fulfilling that need, but she seldom saw him. In Lord Melbourne she found a paternal substitute who was wise, experienced, amusing, even glamorous (Victoria often noted how handsome he looked in some official uniform). Her journal

23

was full of "Lord M," as she called him. She felt "unbounded admiration and affection" for her "excellent Lord Melbourne," her "father," and her "best friend."

In his twin capacities of prime minister and private secretary, Melbourne saw the queen on an average of twice a day, and he usually dined with her in the evenings. In his charming, witty way, he taught her about recent British history, about London "society," and all the people she would have to deal with, and about her duties as queen.

Melbourne realized that Victoria, like most women, had a practical nature, and he did not try to explain to her any high-flown theories of the British constitution. Instead, he wisely talked of actual incidents and the day-to-day business of government. He tried to encourage the spirit of tolerance, not a common quality in young people, especially a tough-willed young woman like Victoria. Arguments, conflicts, fights, should be avoided as far as possible. "Nobody should be troublesome," said Lord Melbourne, "it is the worst thing there is."

The most important of all Melbourne's services to Victoria was that he gave her self-confidence. He sympathized with the ordeals of her childhood and he relieved her fears of inadequacy. Victoria felt uneasy about being short (she was under five feet). Lord M reassured her. She thought that her nose was too large. "Oh," said Lord M, "people with small features never do anything."

The first year of Victoria's reign was an idyll of happiness. She found she enjoyed her regal duties—reading dispatches, writing letters, granting interviews —hard work though it all was. Whether she was at work at her desk, riding in the park, or dining in state, Lord M was always at her side, praising, smiling, explaining. Sometimes she noticed tears in his eyes when he looked at her with a kind and fatherly expression.

In June, 1838, a year after her accession, the coronation took place at Westminster Abbey. It was a glorious occasion, and the splendor of the ancient ceremony was enhanced by the slight figure of the young queen and by the brilliant sunshine—never a dependable commodity in England's damp climate. The Turkish ambassador was so amazed by the show that he forgot where he was, and to the amusement of the crowd stood wide-eyed, murmuring over and over, "All this for a woman!"

Some unfortunate bungling nearly spoiled the ceremony. Nobody thought of holding a rehearsal beforehand, with the result that the officiating bishops sometimes did not know what to do next. The archbishop of Canterbury jammed the ring on the wrong finger (Victoria had a painful time getting it off again later) and he tried to give her the orb when she was

An old engraving of Victoria's coronation in June, 1838. (Charles Phelps Cushing)

already holding it. The ancient Lord Rolle lived up to his name by tripping on the steps up to the throne and rolling all the way down.

Yet these minor mishaps went unnoticed by the great majority, who were enthralled by the ancient spectacle. The whole ceremony lasted many hours; but when she got back to the palace in the evening, the energetic young queen picked up her skirts and ran upstairs to give her spaniel a bath.

Some people felt that the stiff court etiquette made life at Buckingham Palace a boring ordeal. The queen did not approve of the men lingering by themselves after dinner to smoke, drink, and discuss masculine affairs. Male guests were expected to present themselves in the drawing room to "join the ladies" within a few minutes of the end of the meal. The queen would stop and exchange a few words with each guest, as etiquette demanded. Such conversations were often not very interesting: only neutral topics could be discussed. Later, the queen would sit with Lord Melbourne in one corner while the rest of the guests, sighing for their comfortable clubs and amusing friends, stood about trying not to look bored and not daring to leave until it was appropriate to do so.

Victoria herself soon began to find this existence less than fascinating. The first wonderful sensation of independence had faded and she was beginning to show signs of her famous temper. Once or twice she even stormed at Lord Melbourne, though she always

Buckingham Palace, official London residence of the ruling British monarch. At left stands a memorial to Queen Victoria. (Charles Phelps Cushing)

felt sorry afterward. Lord Melbourne would smile and tease her about getting fat, but privately he was sometimes worried by his adored sovereign's signs of selfishness and irritability. Although he was so understanding of Victoria's problems, it was hard for Melbourne to recognize that she needed companions nearer her own age.

For all his careful coaching, Melbourne's influence was sometimes unfortunate. Feeling so protective toward the queen, he unwisely sheltered her from unpleasant facts. He tended always to sympathize with her point of view, though common sense told him she was sometimes wrong. His intense dislike of "trouble" made him slow to deal with dangerous situations.

When Victoria complained about her mother, Melbourne, who disliked the duchess, agreed with her, and though he advised kindness, he made no real attempt to heal the breach between mother and daughter. The duchess in her distant wing of the palace was still under the influence of Sir John Conroy, and when she wished to communicate with Victoria she had to request an interview. In public, mother and daughter behaved with perfect decorum and seemed very fond of each other. In private, an unnatural coldness prevailed. This dangerous situation encouraged court gossip, from which grew a nasty scandal that was to send the queen's popularity plummeting to zero.

Early in 1839, Lady Flora Hastings, the duchess's chief lady-in-waiting, traveled down from Scotland in a carriage with Sir John Conroy. They traveled alone, and the fact was noted and discussed in Victoria's circle. Soon afterward, the queen observed that Lady Flora was growing suspiciously fat. She leaped at once to what seemed the obvious conclusion. Lord Melbourne, who had himself been involved in sensational scandals in the past, agreed with her. The gossip grew louder. Lady Flora was asked to submit to a medical examination. At first she indignantly refused, and when she was finally forced into it, the court doctor could not decide whether she was pregnant or not. A further examination was necessary, which revealed that the maligned Lady Flora was actually a virgin.

This humiliating episode, for which the queen, Lord Melbourne, the court doctor, and a number of others must share the blame, should have been hushed up. Unfortunately, a member of Lady Flora's family, outraged at her treatment, gave the details to the newspapers. The result was a public outcry. The queen and Melbourne were hissed when they went riding. Hostile statements were made in Parliament, and the press kept the scandal boiling with a succession of damning articles. The affair was just beginning to die down when Lady Flora, whose stouter appearance was actually caused by a tumor, died, and again ferocious criticism shook the court. The queen, who was genuinely distressed by the injustice done to her mother's lady-in-waiting, sent a representative to the funeral. Onlookers hurled rocks at the royal carriage.

The wretched affair had one good result, however. The old Duke of Wellington, whose immense prestige as victor over Napoleon and as ex-prime minister made him a national patriarch, was called in to help smooth ruffled feathers. His efforts were unsuccessful, but his observation of the situation at court made him determined to get rid of the man he called that "rascal" Conroy. By playing on Conroy's greed and conceit, the old duke persuaded him to resign from the duchess's service—for a price. From then on, relations between Victoria and her mother steadily improved.

Still, the delights of being a queen all seemed to have vanished in the spring of 1839. Victoria's journal now recorded all the drawbacks: she had no leisure; the work was "very laborious"; court life was dull and nasty. She told Lord Melbourne she felt "unfit for her station." The prime minister hastily reassured her, but the time was coming when he would not be there to encourage the queen in moments of despondency. Victoria could not forever shelter from the hard world of politics behind the comfortable shield provided by Lord Melbourne.

CHAPTER III

"He Is an Angel"

In Great Britain the government remains in power only as long as it can command the support of a majority in Parliament. The prime minister and other members of the cabinet, who form the executive arm of the government, must also be members of Parliament; and all major acts of the government must be approved by Parliament. When the government cannot get a majority in Parliament for its policy, it cannot function and must resign.

By 1839 Lord Melbourne's government had become unpopular. Its supporters in the House of Commons (the lower but more important house) came from a number of different groups, and some of them were breaking away. Several ministers were in favor of resigning at once, hoping that the next parliamentary election would increase their supporters. Melbourne stayed at his post—not because he was fond of power but because he was fond of the queen. If the government resigned, his daily contact with Victoria, the greatest joy of his life, would be broken. As long as his government could struggle on, he meant to continue, and his determination was strengthened by Victoria's distress whenever he mentioned the possibility of resignation.

In May, 1839, the Whigs narrowly escaped defeat by a vote in the House of Commons. The handwriting was on the wall. Even Lord Melbourne agreed that the government could not continue after so damaging a blow to its prestige. He told the queen he must resign, and that she should ask the leader of the Conservative party, Sir Robert Peel, to form an alternative government. The queen cried bitterly. Lord M could not desert her, she protested; but Lord M, as gently as possible, explained that no other course was possible.

Sir Robert Peel's personality was very different from Lord Melbourne's. The son of a self-made industrialist, Peel was very much a man of the new generation. His cold, awkward manner and his provincial accent were a startling contrast to Lord Melbourne's languid aristocratic charm. The queen, of course, was not an objective judge. Her experience with Melbourne had convinced her that the Whigs were the only good

Sir Robert Peel. (Charles Phelps Cushing)

men in government and the Conservatives were a band of dangerous rascals.

The interview with the Conservative leader started quite well, though the disapproving queen noticed that he shuffled his feet (Peel was very shy—hence his reputation for coldness). As the interview drew to a close, Peel mentioned that the queen should make some changes among her ladies of the bedchamber (courtiers officially appointed to attend the queen), who were all Whigs. Victoria bridled. Did he mean to surround her with Conservative spies? she wondered.

Peel's request, however, was a natural one. The government was supposed to have the confidence of the monarch, but everyone knew that Victoria was a fervent Whig supporter. The appointment of some Conservative ladies of the bedchamber would show that the queen was equally prepared to put her trust in a Conservative government. Nevertheless, Victoria was taken by surprise. Previous queens, she said, had not changed their ladies when the government changed. That was true, but as Peel pointed out, the great difference was that previous queens had not usually been reigning sovereigns. (England had not had a queen as sovereign since Queen Anne, over a century earlier.)

So the interview ended without agreement. Peel went off to consult that renowned elder statesman, the Duke of Wellington, while Victoria hastened to put the matter before Lord M. Melbourne thought she was in the right: she need not change the personnel of her household to suit an incoming government. But he added that this was not an important matter, and he advised her to give in to Peel. He knew how dangerous it would be if people thought the queen was a "party politician," and he wanted to be fair to Peel, whom in his easygoing way he quite liked.

Victoria did not take her old friend's advice. When Peel returned for her answer, he found the queen unmoving. On no account would she consider any changes in her household. Would she not give up just a few of her ladies? Peel asked—just those whose husbands were actually Whig members of Parliament? Not one, the queen replied. Peel was thoroughly embarrassed by this display of royal defiance. Finally he stammered that, in the circumstances, he must regretfully decline to form a government.

This was just what Victoria wanted. If the Conservatives would not form a government, Lord Melbourne would have to return, or the country would have no government at all. Melbourne hesitated, but when he explained the situation to his colleagues they all agreed that they could not desert so valiant a young monarch. They might have moderated their enthusiasm if they had known that Peel had not asked for *all* the queen's ladies to be changed, but only *some* of them. For Victoria, whether deliberately or not, had led Lord Melbourne to believe that her whole house-

A portrait of Victoria during the early years of her reign. (Charles Phelps Cushing)

hold was at stake. Her comment on Peel's original request had been, "Such trickery." Others might have thought that her own conduct was not entirely straightforward.

At any rate, the Bedchamber Crisis, as it came to be called, thus ended happily—for Victoria—with the renewal of her partnership with Lord Melbourne. (Nobody would have been more surprised than the Whig prime minister to learn that his government was to last another two years.) And Lord M was as kind, as helpful, as affectionate as ever. Everything would go on perfectly, just as before. Or would it?

In October, 1839, an important visitor was expected at court: Prince Albert of Saxe-Coburg-Gotha. His influence on Queen Victoria was to be far greater even than Lord Melbourne's. Victoria well knew that this young man had been groomed as her future husband. Nothing definite had been decided, but on his one previous visit, three and a half years before, she had declared that the prospect of marrying him was very pleasing to her. Still, three and a half years is a long time in the life of a young woman, and much had changed in the meantime. She could only dimly remember Albert's handsome face. As his arrival drew nearer, doubts crowded in upon her.

To her uncle, King Leopold, she wrote anxiously that she felt "a *great* repugnance" to getting married. The country, she was sure, did not want to see her married yet. She impressed upon him that she *"never gave any* [promise]" to marry Albert.

Leopold received this evidence of cold feet calmly, relying on Albert's presence to strike the necessary spark in his self-willed niece. Events soon proved the wisdom of this policy.

Albert arrived on October 10, soon after dusk had fallen over Windsor Castle. Victoria stood on the stairs to greet him. She looked into the dark eyes set in the pale, handsome face, and suddenly all her doubts vanished. Later that evening she recorded her feelings in her journal: "It was with some emotion that I beheld Albert, who is *beautiful*." The queen was in love.

On the surface, Albert and Victoria had several things in common. They were born within a few months of each other, and both had lost a parent in early childhood. Albert's education, like Victoria's, was sketchy, though he did spend some time at a German university.

Nevertheless, the differences between them were greater than the similarities. Victoria was high-spirited and impetuous; Albert was reserved and cautious. Victoria reacted emotionally to events—in effect, she thought with her heart. Albert always tried to consider everything in the cool spirit of reason—he thought with his head. The name of Albert's elder brother, Ernest, would have suited the younger brother better. Ernest was a disreputable character,

Windsor Castle, the royal residence where Victoria greeted Prince Albert in 1839. (Charles Phelps Cushing)

Albert, Prince Consort of England, in 1840. (The Mansell Collection, London)

while Albert was sober, hardworking, and high-principled.

In possessing these traits, Albert typified the outstanding virtues of the Victorian age. Of course he was not perfect; indeed, he was narrow-minded about some matters, and his sense of humor was rather weak. But his many gifts outweighed his faults, and he was intelligent. Above all, the key to Albert's character was his devotion to duty. Great Britain was fortunate that a man of his integrity and skill was to devote his life to the service of the British monarchy.

Not only was Albert a wise and good man, he was, in his youth, unusually good-looking: "very, very handsome," said the sober Walter Bagehot, much impressed. It is not surprising that Victoria, a great admirer of good looks, fell head over heels in love with him so quickly. Within four days of his arrival she shyly proposed marriage (as Albert was of inferior rank, he could not propose to her).

Victoria was, and always remained, passionately in love with Albert. Were Albert's feelings equally strong? He wrote to Baron Stockmar that the day of his engagement was the happiest of his life, and Albert would not have lied; but his words lack the intensity of Victoria's. His was a more serious, inward-looking character, and his deepest feelings were not easily expressed. However, his love, though genuine, was not yet deep. It was to grow, day by day, over the years, and the political motives that certainly drove him toward marriage with the Queen of England were to be swamped by the all-enveloping love of a wonderfully successful marriage.

The announcement of the engagement was not greeted with enthusiasm by the British people. They disliked the idea of a foreign upstart prince marrying their queen, and Parliament fixed Albert's state income at a lower figure than he (and Victoria) felt reasonable. Also, Albert was uneasy about Victoria's dependence on Lord Melbourne and the Whigs, and he believed that the resentment of the Conservatives accounted for Parliament's hostile attitude toward his income. When Lord Melbourne's secretary was appointed secretary to the prince, against Albert's wishes, he feared that he too was being made a tool of the Whig party. His desires were disregarded again over the question of the honeymoon. Albert wanted a longish honeymoon at Windsor. "Impossible," the queen replied. Albert must not forget that "I am the Sovereign..."

Albert was already aware that difficulties were to be expected when the younger son of a minor German duke married the sovereign of a great power. It seemed that Victoria meant to wear the trousers in the family—a daunting prospect for any bridegroom.

With Albert back in Germany, Victoria too felt the strains common in any engagement when the partners are separated. His return on February 8, 1840, put her, as she said, "at ease about everything." Two

"HE IS AN ANGEL"

days later they were married. Both were under twenty-one.

How blissful were the first weeks of marriage! Breakfasting with Albert, who looked "manly and perfect" in a black velvet jacket; long rides with Albert in Windsor Park; even longer conversations—there was so much to talk about—and, in the evening, endless dancing with Albert. "He is an angel," she told her uncle, King Leopold, who could justly congratulate himself on the successful completion of his plan.

The object of Victoria's lavish affection soon found his existence somewhat less than perfect. He had nothing to do. The queen discussed public business with Lord Melbourne and private business with Baroness Lehzen. She would not talk to Albert about politics, partly because she was jealous of her constitutional position ("I am the Sovereign") and partly because, as she said, "when I am with the Prince I prefer talking on other subjects."

While she read and signed official papers, Albert stood by, ready to pass the blotting paper. He was a fair-minded man and recognized that Melbourne was devoted to the queen's interests, but he felt that he might perform a more important task than simply passing the blotting paper!

On the whole, Albert got along well with Lord Melbourne, who treated him with consideration and seemed not to resent the loss of Victoria's deepest affection. Baroness Lehzen was a worse problem. Albert

45

was naturally upset when he discovered that Victoria would consult with Lehzen on matters that she would not mention to him. The baroness, padding about Windsor Castle on her secret domestic missions, seemed to Albert a formidable obstacle to the success of his marriage. Lehzen's writing paper was headed with a drawing of a locomotive and the words "I am coming." Albert hoped that the motto might soon be changed to "I am going."

"I am only the husband, and not the master in the house," he complained to a friend in Germany. He was not cut out to be an idle courtier; his talents and energy demanded a more serious occupation.

After a few months Victoria became pregnant. Her feelings about the forthcoming birth, like her feelings on many other subjects, were mixed. Though she was to have a very large family, she hated the ordeal of childbirth, and often complained that no man could ever understand the horrors of what she called the shadow side of marriage. (Anesthetics were not available until later in her reign.) Babies were unattractive creatures, she thought, though she became fonder of them as they grew older.

One result of her pregnancy was that Albert's responsibilities increased. He was given a desk next to the queen's, and was allowed to read state dispatches. Despite Lehzen, he carried out some reforms in the running of the royal household, with beneficial results to the royal finances.

"HE IS AN ANGEL"

Albert's orderly mind rebelled against a system in which one government department cleaned the outside of the windows of Buckingham Palace while another department cleaned the inside. (As they never worked together, the windows were always dirty.) Then there was the question of the partly burned candles, collected every evening and replaced by new ones. Albert discovered that one of the servants was making a fine profit out of the sale of old candles. This was stopped. People might laugh at Albert's economies, but their total effect in reducing expenditure was impressive.

Public confidence in the prince was growing. Because childbirth was a more dangerous experience than it is today, it was necessary to choose a regent to reign if the queen died. Parliament argued heatedly over candidates (some members wanted the queen's mother), but in the end Albert was appointed.

Happily, this safeguard was not required, for Princess Vicky (who later became the wife of Frederick III of Germany) was born safely in November, 1840. Whatever the queen's feelings about children, the public was delighted with the young family. The Lady Flora Hastings affair and the Bedchamber Crisis were forgotten, and the popularity of the queen rose even higher when a young man, undoubtedly mad, tried to shoot her while she was out driving in her carriage. (It was the first of many such attempts, but fortunately the would-be assassins of Victorian England

Above, a painting of the royal family about 1846. Right, Prince Albert in his middle years. (Charles Phelps Cushing)

were very poor gunmen, and the only time the queen was even slightly injured was when a demented soldier struck her with a stick.) Though shaken, the queen courageously continued her drive. By the time her carriage returned to the palace it was surrounded by an excited crowd who tossed their hats in the air and cheered the queen until she was deafened.

Victoria's dislike of childbirth did not stop her having children. During the first seventeen years of her marriage no less than nine royal babies were born. Within a few months of Vicky's arrival, the queen, to her annoyance, became pregnant again. This time, to the delight of everyone, the child was a boy, called Albert, nicknamed "Bertie," later Prince of Wales and the future King Edward VII.

Soon after Bertie was born, a full-scale row broke out in the royal nursery. Albert, worried by the frailty of Princess Vicky, blamed Lehzen's management. In private he exploded with bitterness: "Lehzen is a crazy, common, stupid intriguer, obsessed with lust of power." He had never yet complained about Lehzen to Victoria, but this time he could not keep silent. Victoria lost her temper, and they quarreled fiercely. It ended when Albert stalked from the room, leaving Victoria in tears.

The quarrel was not easily healed, but gradually the queen came to realize that Albert's grievances were reasonable ones. Thereafter Lehzen's influence diminished, and one day in 1842 she quietly packed her bags and left for her native Germany, never to return. She did not say good-bye to the queen because she wanted to spare her a harrowing scene. Whatever her faults, Lehzen's unselfish loyalty to Victoria was no common quality.

By the time Lehzen departed, Lord Melbourne too had left the scene. After two difficult years, Prince Albert could at last feel that he was the master as well as the husband in the house.

CHAPTER IV

A Happy Family

"Lord Melbourne is looking as old as the hills," remarked a lady of the court in 1841. While the queen thought him as handsome as ever, the fact was that the prime minister and his government were nearing the end of their political road. They had staggered on for two more years since the Bedchamber Crisis, but now a storm was brewing over the Corn Laws, which governed the all-important price of bread. Lord Melbourne knew that whatever political course he steered, the violence of the storm alone would be enough to blow him out of office.

This time, at least, he would not be leaving the queen alone and helpless. Although Melbourne privately thought that Prince Albert was a rather priggish young man, he had come to appreciate the prince's fine qualities. So, betraying no jealousy of the person who had drawn Victoria's love away from himself, Melbourne had been coaching the prince to take on the role of the queen's close adviser.

The inevitable defeat in a parliamentary vote came in May of 1841. Lord Melbourne had two alternatives: he could resign immediately and hand over the reins to Peel and the Conservatives, or he could call for a general election to select a new House of Commons, the result of which would determine which party formed the government. The queen wanted an election in the hope that the Whigs might win. Lord Melbourne knew they had no chance, but he gave in to the queen's wish. The results justified his pessimism, for the Whigs were soundly defeated.

Victoria took the blow more calmly than she had in 1839, and Lord Melbourne tried to ease the grief of parting, though he admitted that "the proudest as well as the happiest part" of his life ended with his departure from the queen's service. Victoria cried gently and clung to his hand. As graceful as ever, Lord M bowed himself out of the chamber, and out of her life.

The Conservative government that took office under Sir Robert Peel in 1841 was unusually talented. No less than five of the ministers either had been or would be prime ministers (including W. E. Gladstone, who joined the cabinet in 1843). Peel himself, with his outstanding gift for administration and tremendous capacity for work, proved to be one of the best prime ministers of the century. During the five years that his government lasted, it compiled a splendid record of administrative improvements and social reforms.

Once Peel got over his initial shyness, the queen discovered that she did like him after all. Albert's influence helped, for he and Peel were very similar in many ways. Like Albert, Peel was serious, high-minded, very capable, and hardworking. He seemed to be just the sort of man who would appeal to Victoria. And so he did—though she was also attracted by less respectable and more romantic types like Lord Melbourne or Benjamin Disraeli.

Economic policy was really Peel's chief interest. He had something of Albert's instinctive distrust of the old landed aristocracy and preferred the new class of earnest, enterprising men who believed in material progress. In addition, Albert shared with Peel a belief that social problems should be the business of the government, though perhaps Peel would not have gone so far as Albert did in a speech in 1848: "I conceive that one has . . . a *Duty* to perform towards the great mass of the working classes." The suggestion that social welfare should be a political matter was then a very advanced idea. Albert further endeared himself to the poorer section of society by the interest he took in housing. He himself helped to plan houses for workers' families in London—an activity that filled the great Whig magnates with amazement.

Lord Melbourne had never concerned himself with the problems caused by the Industrial Revolution. He did not worry much about the overworked and underfed laborers who thronged the grimy streets of growing factory towns in the English Midlands. Nor were trade and manufacturing among the subjects that gained Lord Melbourne's closest attention. But under the combined influence of Sir Robert Peel and Prince Albert, Queen Victoria was learning about many things she had hardly considered before.

Victoria was always sympathetic toward the unfortunate, and she was shocked by the little she saw of the industrial slums. The very worst places she never did see, for her advisers deliberately prevented it, but she did visit hospitals and even jails. She ordered expenses at court to be reduced because luxury in the palace made such an unpleasant contrast with poverty in the slums. The ladies of the court were told to wear only English lace to help the domestic industry—not a great hardship as the English product was only slightly inferior to the lace of Brussels or Paris.

The plight of individuals always touched the queen, and numberless widows and orphans received unsolicited presents from the royal purse. She was surprisingly tolerant of people in trouble, even criminals. When she was told that one of the footmen was drunk and incompetent, her only comment was, "Poor man."

Famine in Ireland was "too terrible" to think about. Victoria's fondness for humble cottage life—so different from her own existence—heightened her compassion for suffering peasants. But when the peasants dramatized their grievances by setting fire to haystacks and attacking their landlords, it was quite a different matter. The specter of revolution haunted the queen, as it has haunted many other monarchs in history.

Chartism, the militant working-class movement that demanded such reforms as "one man—one vote," aroused only fear and anger in Victoria. She did not understand the complaints of the Chartists; Lord Melbourne had always dismissed such people as "troublemakers," and in this case his influence still lingered. Her attitude was understandable. In 1848 revolutions broke out in nearly every major country in Europe, and many people believed that the great Chartist meeting planned for London in that year might start a revolution in England. The staunch Victoria was for once reduced to shivering fright. She and her children were hustled out of the city for safety, but the alarm proved exaggerated. The Chartist meeting was peaceful, and the only injury was suffered by a speaker who fell off his wooden soapbox.

Although the Queen of England possessed several residences, none of them was very suitable for a young couple with a growing family. Buckingham Palace was too public and short of bedrooms; so was Brighton

Pavilion, the exotic Oriental palace built by George IV. Windsor Castle was large and magnificent, but there are distinct disadvantages to living in a medieval fortress. Victoria wanted to live somewhere more comfortable and less public.

Sir Robert Peel suggested the Isle of Wight, which lies off the south coast of England. The royal couple inspected a site at Osborne, liked it, and decided to build there. In 1846 they moved in.

Osborne was a great success. "Our island home," as Prince Albert fondly called it, was secluded and pleasantly rural; yet, thanks to that very recent improvement in communications, the railroads, it was only a few hours' journey from London. At Osborne the queen and the prince could ride through the woods and fields with no attendants—an unusual experience for them. Albert was an enthusiastic gardener, and he laid out shrubberies, terraces, and flower beds on the grounds. He imported the monkey-puzzle tree (Chile pine), which soon became very popular in England, as did another of his innovations, the Christmas tree. The prince was a keen farmer too, and started a farm at Osborne. (He had another farm at Windsor where, to his great satisfaction, he once won first prize for pig breeding.)

In the summer the queen could go bathing—in a bathing suit that covered a great deal more than a modern evening dress. Her method of entering the water was something like a state procession. She

Osborne House on the Isle of Wight, favorite royal residence of Victoria and Albert. The Queen died here in 1901. (Charles Phelps Cushing)

changed inside a bathing machine (a shed on wheels), which was towed to the water by women (men were not allowed anywhere near it). Once in the water, curtains shrouded the steps which the queen descended. Only when the sea covered her up to her neck was the bathing machine withdrawn.

Partly to please her Scottish subjects, the queen often spent her summer vacation in Scotland. Thanks to Albert's economies there was still money to spend, and they were able to buy Balmoral Castle as their Scottish home.

There Prince Albert enjoyed the mountain scenery, which reminded him of his home, and Victoria came nearest to achieving the simple country life she always wanted. The blunt honesty of the Scots enchanted her, and the good hunting pleased the prince, who was an excellent marksman. While Albert was out shooting, Victoria would trot round the cottages, chatting with the women and bringing gifts for the sick and the old. It was much more "amusing" than the stately court life of Windsor and Buckingham Palace. What if sophisticated Londoners did think the prince looked rather silly in a kilt? Victoria thought he looked splendid.

The interludes of domestic privacy were brief, and state business could never be ignored. At Balmoral or Osborne, state dispatches would arrive daily, and a cabinet minister was always in attendance. In affairs of state, Albert was by now the dominant partner.

Balmoral Castle, Scotland. (Charles Phelps Cushing)

Indeed, the queen had come to trust his wisdom and rely on his guidance in everything. Even the comments she wrote in her journal sometimes sound like quotations from her husband.

Family life was their great release from the formal behavior that was normally expected of the monarchy. The queen was barred by her position from having really close friends, and Albert, reserved by nature and suspicious of the English aristocracy, made few friends in England.

At least the queen could talk to foreign royalty on an equal footing, and state visits therefore had some advantages. She grew fond of old Louis Philippe of France, and when his subjects removed him from his throne in 1848, it was to England that he came as a refugee. There he was treated as kindly as possible under the rather delicate circumstances. The Russian emperor, with his fierce black eyes and white eyelashes, was crude but kind. He ordered straw from the stables to sleep on, and he made eyes at the prettiest ladies of the court. Victoria was "amused."

Other visitors were less welcome. The king of Hanover, Victoria's uncle, came over to attend a wedding. He was an irritable old fellow and begrudged Prince Albert—the member, as he thought, of a humbler family than his own—his position of precedence at the ceremony. When the time came to sign the marriage register, he pushed himself between the queen and the prince, determined to sign his name before

Albert did. Victoria noticed this stratagem and, when she had signed, she picked up the book, slid swiftly around the table, and handed it directly to Albert. The king of Hanover, to his great annoyance, was outflanked.

This was a time of great happiness for Victoria. She was young and full of spirit, adoring her husband and, despite the unpleasantness of childbirth, proud of her ever-growing family. The nine-year-old Princess Vicky, out riding with her father, looked quite a young lady, the proud mother noted, and Bertie, the Prince of Wales, though rather backward, had "such affectionate feelings, great truthfulness & great simplicity of character." Balmoral was beautiful, Osborne so peaceful; even Buckingham Palace had its charms since Albert had renovated it. Victoria was conscious of her own contentment. "No other queen," she wrote in her journal, "has ever enjoyed what I am fortunate enough to enjoy."

CHAPTER V

Trials and Triumphs of Prince Albert

The Corn Laws, which had helped to bring down Lord Melbourne's government in 1841, were also the cause of Sir Robert Peel's defeat in 1846. As leader of the Conservative party, Peel was committed to maintain the duties on imported grain, but privately he had come to doubt the wisdom of this policy. The potato famines in Ireland finally convinced him that duties must be ended so as to allow the Irish to buy cheaper bread. And his own supporters, urged on by the savage wit of Benjamin Disraeli, turned against him. The government was defeated by a vote in the House of Commons, and Peel resigned.

It seemed so long ago that the queen had said good-bye to Lord Melbourne and received his successor with gloomy foreboding. And now it was the noble

Sir Robert, who had become a devoted friend and made her feel "so safe," who was to be taken away. It was not good for the country, she thought, and it was most upsetting to her (the two things were often closely connected in the queen's mind). She was thankful that she now had a refuge from such blows: "When one is so happy & blessed in one's home life," she wrote, "politics . . . must take only a 2nd. place."

The repeal of the Corn Laws split the Conservative party in two. Some Conservatives, like William Gladstone (the future Liberal prime minister) stuck to Peel. A larger, though less distinguished number, including Benjamin Disraeli (the future Conservative prime minister) broke away. The old Whig party, too, had broken up, and as a result of these changes party politics became very confused. The next twenty years were to witness many shifts in party alliances, temporary coalitions, and other make-do measures. This state of confusion was to last until 1868, when party politics were again polarized around the two great leaders, Gladstone for the Liberal party and Disraeli for the Conservative party.

In the early Victorian period, the most remarkable man on the political scene, not excepting Peel, was Lord Palmerston. Except during the years of Peel's ministry, Palmerston was a member of the government almost continuously from 1807 to 1865. For much of that time he was either foreign secretary or prime minister. It was his direction of British foreign policy that earned him his greatest fame and, incidentally, brought him into sharp conflict with Prince Albert and the queen.

"Pam," as he was called, was immensely popular. He was, like Lord Melbourne, a Whig of the old school—easygoing, affable, confident, and good-looking. His liking for horses, fancy waistcoats, and pretty women endeared him to the masses (though not to Victoria), and his high spirits and self-assurance suited the mood of a confident and expanding nation. He was what the British used to call a "sportsman": he once paid out of his own pocket for the legal defense of a man who had tried to murder him.

Palmerston was also an astute politician and a bold statesman. His casual exterior concealed a keen practical brain and great energy. Perhaps his chief fault was that he believed in speaking frankly and seldom bothered about the niceties required by international diplomacy. While Palmerston called a spade a spade, there are times when diplomats should call a spade an excavatory implement. If he thought the French were not to be trusted, or the Austrians were behaving like a lot of old women, Palmerston said so. In the courts of Europe his dispatches arrived like an artillery barrage. The Prussians made up a rhyme about him:

> If the devil had a son
> Surely he'd be Palmerston.

As a member of the cabinet, the foreign secretary was responsible to his colleagues and to the prime minister, but Palmerston had a habit of making his own decisions, and explaining them afterwards. The prime minister did not like this behavior, but Pam was too powerful to be fired. The queen and Prince Albert liked it even less.

Victoria had the right to be consulted about all government decisions, and she regarded foreign policy as her special interest. Many European heads of state were her close relatives, and they were quick to complain to her when they felt they had been injured or insulted by the British foreign secretary. But Palmerston, she complained, persisted in acting as if she did not exist.

Like most monarchs, Queen Victoria believed in preserving the established order. Palmerston's sympathies, however, often lay with people who were trying to assert their independence against foreign governments. Thus, he supported the nationalist revolt of the Italians against the Austrian Empire, while the queen—to be more accurate, one should always say Albert *and* the queen—supported the Austrian government.

To avoid royal arguments, Palmerston sometimes issued dispatches to British ambassadors abroad without first submitting them for the queen's approval, and when she complained, he justified himself by saying that she always kept them too long. Sometimes he would completely change the wording of a dispatch *after* the queen had approved it. Victoria protested, and Palmerston apologized sweetly, but three weeks later the same thing would happen again. By 1850, the palace and the foreign office were not on speaking terms.

In the end, Palmerston went too far. When Louis Napoleon came to power in France by a coup d'état, in 1851, Palmerston told the French ambassador that the new regime had his full approval. Now, if the foreign secretary expresses approval of an important event abroad, he is supposed to represent the views of the British government; but on this occasion the government was by no means ready to give its approval so promptly. The prime minister, Lord John Russell, was outraged, and plucked up his courage to demand Palmerston's resignation.

Palmerston soon had his revenge on Lord John Russell. Within two months, his powerful influence in Parliament brought down the Russell government. "Tit for tat" said Pam cheerfully to his former chief.

In the long quarrel over the sovereign's rights in foreign affairs, Palmerston was not the only one at fault. Many people had noticed that the prince and the queen "labored under the curious mistake . . . that they have a right to control, if not to direct, the foreign policy of England." That was the view of another foreign secretary, Lord Clarendon, who also found royal interference irksome at times.

The truth was that the powers of the crown in foreign affairs were not clear-cut. Albert never truly grasped all the subtleties of the constitutional rights of the crown and, partly as a result of his influence, Victoria always tried to play a larger part in international affairs than Lord Palmerston, for one, was willing to concede her. Most ministers showed a commendable tolerance toward Her Majesty's intrusions into affairs that were not strictly her concern.

The clash with Palmerston was one of personalities as well as politics. Two men more different than Palmerston and the prince could hardly be imagined. But in future years, rows with Pam were fewer and less fierce. There was much in his blunt assertion of British interests abroad that appealed to the hearty patriotism of Queen Victoria.

In Victorian England the word "progress" was one to raise the spirits. People were caught up in the rush of scientific and industrial advance, which had brought such revolutionary improvements in society. "Progress" was certain and unstoppable, and, of course, thoroughly desirable. The earnest new generation, of which Prince Albert was in so many ways typical, had no doubts about that. Hard work and prayer were the watchwords of the time. By such simple means, men thought, society—even human nature—could be improved. This was the optimistic message of the Great Exhibition of 1851.

TRIALS AND TRIUMPHS OF PRINCE ALBERT

International expositions are very commonplace today, but a century ago the idea was fairly new. It was probably the prince himself who had the idea of turning an annual exhibition of English products into a great international affair. Certainly it would never have happened without his powers of organization and fund-raising.

The first task was to secure the support of British industry. Hearing that the prince was backing the project, most manufacturers promised to send their goods. Foreign governments were approached, and the colonies promised to send exhibits. Raising capital was a trickier problem. Parliament refused state support, and most of the money had to be extracted from private subscribers. A vast amount of work was involved in all this, and Albert was its driving force. Often he got up well before dawn and returned long after dark. It is not surprising that Victoria noticed he looked "very ill of an evening."

Opposition to Prince Albert's scheme was widespread and much of it absurd. One of the greatest difficulties concerned the site. Albert was determined on London's Hyde Park. Noisy protests were raised by fashionable members of society who were accustomed to go horseback riding there. Their recreation would be impossible, these fortunate folk complained, with crowds of people milling about. And some of those crowds would probably be undesirables: they would rob the houses of the wealthy and seduce their maid-

Chief attraction of London's Great Exhibition of 1851 was the huge Crystal Palace, which measured over 1,800 feet.

servants. Such a threat to private property was intolerable!

The exhibition building itself—a glass-structured palace so large that it enclosed several lofty elms growing on the site—aroused jeers and warnings of doom. A strong gale would blow it down; a loud noise would break it; it would be too hot or too cold, and so on. Nobody foresaw the one genuine drawback of the Crystal Palace: birds roosting overhead in the elms threatened to cover everything with their droppings. But how to get the birds out? The aged Duke of Wellington once more came to the rescue of his country. "Try sparrow-hawks, ma'am," he told the queen. It worked.

Engineers said the galleries of the Crystal Palace would collapse; economists forecast a desperate food shortage; and doctors feared foreigners would bring in an epidemic. With a sigh, Prince Albert got on with the job.

When the exhibition finally opened on May 1, 1851, all but the most reactionary critics were silenced. It was a glittering success. The basis of the exhibition was machinery and raw materials, from Britain and the British Empire and from foreign countries also. Among the arts and crafts some strange and ingenious objects appeared: a garden seat made of coal (English); a group of stuffed frogs, one holding an umbrella (Germany); champagne made from rhubarb, and so on.

The queen and her family attended the opening ceremony. She wore for the first time the dazzling Koh-i-Noor diamond, acquired from India two years before. It was a wonderful moment, "the *happiest, proudest* day in my life," she wrote to King Leopold. "Albert's dearest name is immortalised with this *great* conception." To enter that "blazing arch of lucid glass," as the novelist William Thackeray described the Crystal Palace, was rather like entering church, and at least one cabinet minister was moved to tears at the sight of this great monument to international peace.

The Great Exhibition marked the apex of Albert's career and popularity, and it symbolized the achievements of an era of peace and prosperity. But unfortunately history is full of ironies. Within three years, Britain was at war, and Prince Albert was denounced in the public press as a traitor to his adopted country.

CHAPTER VI

War and Alliances

Nineteenth-century Europe was beset by a complex of problems which were known collectively as the Eastern Question. The heart of the matter was the weakness of the two old empires of Austria and Turkey, which between them controlled all of southeastern Europe.

The decline of a great power always creates a political vacuum, which must be filled either by another great power or by new national groups. Thus the Austrian Empire was shortly to lose a limb when the Italian nationalist movement waged a successful war to create an independent Italy.

For Britain, the decline of the Ottoman Empire of Turkey was a serious matter which raised many ominous questions for the future. For good political

73

reasons, Turkey was called the Sick Man of Europe. It was no longer capable of controlling its ramshackle empire, which stretched deep into Europe and included part of Greece and the Balkan countries (Bulgaria, Rumania, Siberia, and so on). The Turkish government was hopelessly old-fashioned, and it was headed by a succession of sultans who were either feeble, underage, or downright insane.

The British had no special liking for the oppressive and corrupt administration of the Turks, and they realized that sooner or later it must fall; yet many British statesmen tried very hard to preserve it from collapse. The vacuum created by Turkey's decline would be filled, they feared, not by the rising nationalist movement in the Balkan countries, but by the menacing power of Russia. Turkey itself was no threat to British interests—but Russia was. If the Russians controlled the Turkish capital of Constantinople, they would dominate the whole Middle East and threaten the security of British India. These assumptions directed the actions of British ministers in the mid-nineteenth century.

The crisis of 1853 sprang from Russia's claims to "protect" the Christian subjects of the Turkish Empire (the Turks, of course, were Muslims). When the Turks refused to accept Russia's demands, the armies of the czar marched into Turkish territory. Nobody wanted war—not the Turks, not the British or their allies the French, not even the Russians. But the Turkish government was foolish, the Russian government impetuous, the British feeble, and the French inexperienced. War, a thoroughly pointless war, became inevitable.

At the beginning of the crisis, Victoria admitted that she could not see that it mattered who held Constantinople, the Turks or the Russians. She soon changed her mind. By October, 1853, when Turkey declared war on Russia, the queen was beginning to think that force was necessary to convince the czar that Britain would not stand by and watch him swallow up Constantinople.

The British public was spoiling for a fight. Britain had not been engaged in a major war since the defeat of Napoleon at Waterloo in 1815, and the crude patriotism of Victorian England was easily turned into aggressiveness. The Russians were unpopular, and the plight of the Turks, whose navy was demolished at one blow by a vastly superior Russian fleet, helped to build up hatred against the czar and all his works. The country was in a state bordering on hysteria and, late in 1853, for no good reason, public opinion suddenly turned violently against Prince Albert.

Prince Albert never really commanded the love of the British people. Respect, yes. But affection? No —for he seemed too cold and unfeeling. As he admitted, he was "not of a demonstrative nature." However, it was not his fault that he was German, and he could not hope to alter the British dislike of foreigners.

The wave of public hostility was set off by the resignation of Lord Palmerston from the government. In fact, Palmerston resigned because he disagreed with the prime minister's proposals for parliamentary reform, but the reason was not announced. The public knew that his was the loudest anti-Russian voice in the cabinet, and thought, quite wrongly, that Albert must be pro-Russian. The prince, it was said, had forced Pam's resignation.

The popular press launched a series of attacks on Albert that were ferocious, tasteless, and completely false. Bawdy rhymes, too crude to be funny, were shouted in the streets. A rumor went round that the prince had been accused of treason, and an ignorant crowd gathered to watch him being taken to the Tower of London in irons.

Albert bore it all stoically, though he wrote privately that "the nonsense and lies, which the public have had to swallow with respect to my humble person . . . have really exceeded anything I could have imagined." The queen's language, as usual, was less restrained. She was "enraged and indignant" at such "shameful and infuriating slanders."

When Parliament met in January, 1854, the leaders of all parties made speeches condemning the outrageous behavior of the newspapers and praising the prince's loyalty and patriotism. This brought people to their senses, and the attacks ceased as suddenly as they had begun.

WAR AND ALLIANCES

As war drew nearer, the queen became more and more military-minded. When the prime minister talked of patching things up, she rebuked him sharply. It was necessary to fight now to avoid worse troubles in the future, she said. Amid scenes of public rejoicing, in March of 1854, the Crimean War began.

Centuries earlier, the king of England had traditionally led his armies into battle—Edward III at Crécy; Henry V at Agincourt; even old George II at Dettingen, not much more than a hundred years before. Victoria may have remembered these great events as she waved her white handkerchief to the ships carrying the army to the distant Crimean peninsula of Russia. Of course, war was dreadful; no one was more sympathetic to grieving widows than Queen Victoria. All the same, war was glorious, too. There was no finer way for a man to die than on the battlefield, and her heart beat fiercely as, with flags flying, bands playing, and guns firing a royal salute, the ships pulled away in the gray dawn light. The blood of her ancestors stirred in the queen's veins, and Albert, as he stood beside her, must have thought, not for the first time, that being a British sovereign was more than a matter of signing state papers.

In her eagerness to hear news of the progress of the war, Victoria became nervous and overwrought. She pestered every returning officer for information, and worked off nervous energy by knitting gloves and scarves for the soldiers, or writing endless letters to the families of those men who had died. Albert was equally energetic. He rapidly made himself a master of every aspect of war administration, and in a little over two years he wrote enough notes and memoranda to fill fifty large volumes.

Britain was proud of her reputation as "the workshop of the world," but supplying the Crimean army soon began to strain her powers of manufacture and organization. Communications and administration were badly bungled. Ammunition was sent out that did not fit the rifles; a shipment of boots were all for the left foot.

The story of the Crimean War is a sorry tale of error and incompetence, both in battle and behind the lines. Part of the trouble was lack of experience. It had been a long time since the Napoleonic Wars and, in the interval, weapons and equipment had changed. The generals were all elderly men (the commander in chief was nearly seventy) and their military ideas were out of date. Dreadful mistakes in tactics were made. When the famous Light Brigade (of cavalry) was ordered to charge the Russian artillery along an exposed valley, half of them, not surprisingly, were killed. As a French general who was looking on remarked, it was magnificent, but it was not war (*"C'est magnifique mais ce n'est pas la guerre"*).

True, mistakes as bad as these had been made in earlier wars; but this time the public was better informed. War correspondents reported directly from the battlefield, and newspapers were widely read. The enthusiasm which greeted the outbreak of war soon turned to indignation and disgust at the terrible sufferings of the soldiers. Reports of ill-equipped hospitals, where the wounded were crowded together in frightful conditions and often left to die without medical attention, were especially horrifying.

The bad management of the war brought down the government in 1855, and by popular demand, Lord Palmerston became prime minister. As the war administration improved, Victoria and Albert had to admit that Pam was a much more agreeable creature as prime minister than he was as foreign secretary.

At the same time, perhaps the most extraordinary Englishwoman of her generation was bringing order out of chaos in the Turkish hospitals where the British wounded lay by the thousands. Florence Nightingale was a slight, feminine person whom the soldiers called "the Lady with the Lamp," because she toured the rows of wounded at night, carrying a lamp, and bringing a few priceless words of comfort to the broken men. Underneath, this gentle, ministering angel was a veritable tiger.

No ordinary woman could have done such a job in those days when respectable women of her social class were not expected to work at anything. Within a few months, she completely reorganized the hospitals. Her willpower and persistence were extraordinary. She charmed, she persuaded, and when blocked by red tape, she acted anyway. Clothing, food, laundry services, sheets, beds, even new buildings, materialized as if by magic. She drove herself unsparingly, and she commanded the same selflessness in her helpers. After the war, when she went on to revolutionize the nursing profession in England, at least one of her devoted disciples suffered a breakdown in health as a result of his relentless efforts on behalf of her ideals.

Reports of Miss Nightingale's work in the Turkish hospitals came to the ears of Victoria. The queen was a little jealous of this war heroine. How she wished she might be a nurse and look after her "noble brave heroes."

Later, these two remarkable women came face-to-face. Victoria was relieved to find that Miss Nightingale was not at all the battle-ax she had expected, and she was immensely pleased to hear stories of the soldiers' devotion to their queen. Miss Nightingale told her of a corporal in a London hospital who had given up his heavy drinking after a royal visit. Victoria was always proud of her ability to reform drunkards, and she was surprisingly tolerant of that weakness in what were called the lower orders of society.

For the ordinary soldier, the phrase "Queen and Country" had real meaning. He truly felt that he fought for the queen—as a person as well as a vague institution. After the war, veterans whom the queen had presented with medals refused to give them up to be engraved, in case the medal they got back was not the same one that the queen's own hand had pinned to their tunic. Victoria heard this story with immense satisfaction. Sentimental gestures such as this appealed to her.

Like many wars, the Crimean War solved no fundamental problems. Russia was checked for the time being, but the "Eastern Question" remained unanswered. One good result was the improved relationship between Britain and France, who had fought as allies against Russia. To cement this new friendship the French emperor Napoleon III was invited to England along with his glamorous empress, Eugénie (who came in crinoline, then a novelty in England).

Napoleon III was one of those romantic, faintly outrageous characters who often attracted Victoria, and the visit was a great success. A state ball, a military review, a visit to the Crystal Palace, concerts, ceremonies, all followed in glittering succession. The French emperor, stroking his waxed mustache, was all Gallic charm, and the empress was "very pretty and very un-common looking." They both behaved "really with the greatest tact," Victoria reported with profound relief to King Leopold.

Next year the visit was returned. Victoria was the first English sovereign to set foot in Paris in over five hundred years. She smiled when the people shouted, *"Vive la Reine!"* and her smile widened when they shouted no less loudly, *"Vive le Prince Albert!"* Sophisticated Parisians may have chuckled at the queen's bonnet (she refused to wear a grander headdress), but Victoria was equally amused by the appearance of some of the people she met, especially one old general with a very red face and huge mustache.

Two years later, this spirit of friendship was suddenly shaken by an unfortunate incident in France. Somebody threw a grenade at the emperor's carriage and, though he was only slightly injured, a great many people were killed. On examination the grenade was found to have been made in England.

Thanks to its relatively liberal form of government, England had the reputation of being a haven for anarchists, revolutionaries, and other political undesirables. The grenade incident confirmed Europe's worst impressions, and the French lodged a strong protest.

So strong was French diplomatic pressure for greater political security that Lord Palmerston was persuaded to introduce in Parliament a bill against conspiracy. Parliament regarded the bill as an infringement of civil liberties, and refusing to be dictated to by France, voted against it by a large majority. Lord Palmerston resigned and a Conservative government took over. It was an odd stroke of fate that Lord Palmerston, who used to bully European governments unmercifully, was defeated for being too subservient to a foreign power.

However, the "whiskered wonder," as his supporters called the aging Palmerston, was back as prime minister the next year (1859), and soon found himself again in conflict with the queen. This time, another aspect of the "Eastern Question" was involved.

The nationalities under Austrian rule were clamoring for independence. In 1859 France made war on Austria-Hungary in support of the nationalist revolt in Italy. Palmerston, though suspicious of Napoleon's motives, supported the Italians. The queen and the prince consort, always opposed to revolutions, supported the "established" power of Austria.

Fortunately, the war soon ended, and on other international questions the queen and Palmerston often thought alike. The prime minister even won the queen's sympathy in some of his difficulties—for instance, when he was attacked in Parliament by a member of his own party, a "strange and excitable" man, as Queen Victoria described W. E. Gladstone.

CHAPTER VII

An End and a Beginning

Victoria's eighth child, Prince Leopold, was born in April, 1853. The birth was a less unpleasant experience than usual, thanks to the recent invention of anesthetics. Many people thought that it was somehow wrong or unnatural to soothe the suffering of childbirth, but Victoria was enthusiastic: "That blessed Chloroform," she reported, was "soothing, quieting & delightful beyond measure."

The little prince was a sickly child, and he turned out to be a sufferer from a sinister affliction, hemophilia, or the bleeding disease, which prevents the blood from clotting and makes the slightest scratch or bruise highly dangerous. Hemophilia is hereditary, and while only men suffer from it, women can transmit it to their children. Since Albert did not have it,

Victoria must have been the carrier (though it had not appeared before on either side of her family). In addition to Leopold, three daughters proved to be transmitters, and through them the disease came to afflict every royal family in Europe.

Worry over Prince Leopold wore down Victoria's nerves; she was always depressed after childbirth and this additional stress made her nervous and irritable. There was a sharp quarrel with Albert. Even the happiest marriages have their ups and downs, and in the case of a woman of Victoria's temperament, "storms" had to be expected occasionally. Albert's usual method of dealing with his wife's outbreaks of temper was to retire to his study in pained silence. From that refuge, he sent her cool and logical notes, pointing out, quite kindly, why she was being foolish and what she should do to improve her behavior in the future. Perhaps this was not the best way of dealing with an emotionally overwrought woman, but sooner or later Victoria's affectionate nature reasserted itself, and Albert's patience made the eventual reconciliation easier.

The queen was not an easy person to live with, but she recognized this fact herself. "My nature," she admitted, "is too passionate" (i.e., "violent"). Every New Year she would resolve to be calmer and more sensible, and Albert would sometimes compliment her on her recent performance: "I can give you a very

AN END AND A BEGINNING

good certificate this time and am pleased to witness with you your own improvement." To the task of "improving" his wife's character, Albert brought the same earnest effort that he brought to improving the administration of Buckingham Palace or the conduct of foreign relations.

As the months and years went by, the tasks and duties of the prince consort (Albert was given that title in 1856) became more and more demanding. Always he seemed to be at work; so much so that the queen worried about his health. Albert did not age well. At forty he looked like fifty or more. He had put on weight and had lost his hair. His complexion was pale, and he often seemed tired. Since his youth he had suffered from a weak stomach, and such minor ailments as colds or toothaches affected him more than other people. He once told Victoria, to her dismay, that he would never survive a serious illness.

Although the royal family was still expanding (Princess Beatrice, the last child, was born in 1857), the older children were almost grown up. Vicky, the eldest and Albert's favorite, had a suitor in 1855. She was not quite fifteen, but princesses traditionally married at an early age. Her admirer, who had been chosen for her some years before, was young Prince Frederick of Prussia (the future emperor of Germany). He came to stay at Balmoral, and after a week's courting, presented the English princess with a sprig of white heather and asked her to be his bride. Vicky, younger but brighter than her future husband, gratefully accepted.

This dramatic family event left Victoria with mixed feelings. Primarily, it was difficult to accept her daughter as a grown woman. Sometimes Vicky seemed grown up, sometimes just a child. And, despite her own marital happiness, Victoria had misgivings about marriage. In those days marriage meant, first and foremost, childbearing. In some of her changeable moods, the queen tended to look upon the young bride as an innocent lamb delivered up for the sacrifice.

Prince Frederick was an amiable young man and certainly an eligible husband. From the political point of veiw, an English alliance with Prussia was highly desirable. But what of the bride's feelings? Was she really in love? Happily, Vicky assured her mother that she was. Queen Victoria hated "political" marriages in which the feelings of the individuals were not considered.

The marriage should not take place, Victoria firmly insisted, until the bride was seventeen. It was a long engagement therefore, and like most long engagements, not free from pitfalls. The press in both England and Prussia was unenthusiastic, and the Prussian court tactlessly suggested that the marriage ought to take place in Berlin. At this, Queen Victoria exploded, declaring that "the assumption of its being

AN END AND A BEGINNING

too much for a Prince Royal of Prussia to *come* over to marry *the Princess Royal of Great Britain* IN England is too *absurd,* to say the least . . . it is not *every* day that one marries the eldest daughter of the Queen of England." After that, there was no more talk of holding the wedding in Prussia.

At times during the long engagement, Victoria almost wished her daughter's wedding was over and done with. The princess now had to be treated as an adult, which meant, among other things, that she dined with her parents in the evenings. Victoria seldom had Albert to herself, for he was busy all day and often away from home attending some public function.

When the day of the wedding finally came, in January of 1858, the queen was again overcome by anxiety. She trembled so much, she said later, that she came out blurred in the wedding photograph (photography was another recent invention). Tears ran down her cheeks as she said good-bye to the young couple. Albert went with them as far as the port, then drove back to Windsor through thick snow to write a long, sorrowful letter to the daughter who had brightened every day for him: "You can hardly know how dear you have always been to me, and what a void you have left behind in my heart."

Indeed, the bride was soon inundated with letters from England, for her mother wrote almost every day. In an age of great letter writers, Victoria excelled, and her warnings, advice, comfort, and encouragement were redoubled when—much too soon the queen thought—Vicky became pregnant. A year after the wedding, Victoria and Albert became grandparents. The child was the future Emperor William II of Germany, and he was born with a withered arm.

While Victoria's eldest daughter, now settled happily in Berlin, had always been an easy child, affectionate, intelligent, and obedient, the parents had to admit that, by comparison, their eldest son was a slight disappointment. As Prince of Wales and heir to the throne, Bertie had a great future ahead of him. He would fill the highest place in the kingdom, and much was expected of him. But at times his mother wondered whether he had the character for such a position.

Poor Bertie's chief fault was that he was not like Albert. Although far from stupid, he was no scholar, and his marks in subjects like ancient history and classics were extremely bad. He was better at modern military history, but this interest was not encouraged. He was not allowed to go to school with other boys and, at the age of thirteen, he was separated from the brother nearest him in age. So he had no friends or companions. It is surprising that Victoria, remembering her own lonely childhood, allowed this. It was foolish, too, to take away Bertie's young tutor, whom he liked, and to replace him with a dry and narrow-minded scholar whom Bertie loathed.

AN END AND A BEGINNING

Prince Albert did not admire the English aristocracy with their horses, cards, and women. He was determined to protect his son from their undesirable influence. But Bertie did not share his father's high-minded interests; he was a sociable and affectionate fellow at heart, and as he grew up, he found the amusements of the aristocracy very much to his liking. Victoria, watching him, saw in her eldest son all the worst qualities of her own uncles, those unsatisfactory sons of George III. She and Albert tried to stamp out these signs and to turn the future Edward VII into a carbon copy of Prince Albert. Of course it could not work, and though they meant well, the attempt was unwise. It made the childhood of the future king unnecessarily harsh. It speaks well for Bertie's truly amiable disposition that he was always absolutely loyal to his mother. And when, many years after Albert's death, the Prince of Wales started to speak of his father at an official banquet, he broke down in tears and could not go on.

For despite Bertie's educational problems and an occasional quarrel, it was a truly happy family. Albert, cold and reserved in public, was at his best among his children; his family was his chief pleasure, and only among its members were his kindness and good humor fully revealed. His devotion to the queen, whose happiness he always put before his own, and the warm trust between him and all the children made life at home, as Victoria herself said, "bright and happy."

Albert was always the one who thought up expeditions, parties, games—all kinds of fun to relieve the strict routine of royal existence. The queen's journal is full of these incidents: Albert playing with the baby; Albert teaching the girls to dance, throwing a party for the servants, or organizing a family holiday; Albert walking with Victoria through Cambridge in disguise, chatting to the Highlanders at Balmoral, planning a toy house at Osborne; Albert riding through the fields in a "wide-awake" hat; Albert skating on Windsor pond; Albert out shooting in his scarlet boots. For the queen, it was impossible to imagine life without him. Victoria sometimes prayed that she might die before he did.

Early in 1861 the queen's mother, the old Duchess of Kent, died. Thanks to Albert's influence, former quarrels had been forgotten many years before, and the duchess's old age had been a happy one. Her death was sudden, and Victoria took it badly. When Victoria sorted out her mother's papers, she found many affectionate notes about herself, and remembering her hardness twenty years before, she was overcome by guilt, sorrow, and remorse.

The queen fell into a state of melancholy, sitting by a window for hours and crying. Albert, who was feeling the strains of overwork, could not snap her out of her grief. Not until autumn did she recover, and by then, Albert was looking very tired and ill. Even Victoria, who despite Albert's baldness and obesity

This photograph, taken in March, 1861, shows Queen Victoria with Prince Albert. The Prince Consort died in December of that year. (Gernsheim Collection)

still thought him the handsomest man in the world, had to admit that he looked terrible.

The prince caught a cold and could not get rid of it. Worse still, he could not sleep. The Portuguese royal family had just been wiped out in an epidemic of typhoid, and Albert grieved over the young king, who had always been a favorite of his.

More bad news arrived in November. The Prince of Wales, who was attending Cambridge University, had somehow evaded his guardians long enough to enjoy a brief affair with a woman. For Albert, this came as a terrible shock. It threatened all that he and Victoria had done to make the monarchy the object of respect. It recalled again the bad old days of George III and the disreputable royal dukes.

Sternly ignoring his aches and pains, Albert hurried up to Cambridge. He returned in a more peaceful frame of mind, for Bertie had been frank and open with his father. But Albert was now really sick. His back and legs ached, and he felt feverish and could not sleep a wink. These symptoms were variously diagnosed by the doctors as rheumatism and influenza. Even so, the prince was not strictly confined to bed. He felt restless, and was allowed to wander about the draughty passages of Windsor, shifting his bed from room to room as the mood took him. The doctors assured the queen that there was no cause for worry.

AN END AND A BEGINNING

On November 28, news reached England of an ominous incident at sea. The British ship *Trent*, on her way to England from Cuba, was intercepted by a United States warship. The Civil War was raging in America, and the United States government had learned that the *Trent* carried four representatives of the Confederate States on their way to London and Paris. Despite British protests, the four Southerners were forcibly removed. This action was, of course, illegal, and the British government was naturally indignant. Some ministers sympathized with the South, and an angry message was drafted for the United States government, demanding an apology and the immediate release of the prisoners. Late on the evening of November 30, the draft of the message reached Windsor for the royal approval.

Albert was now so ill that he could hardly hold a pen, but when he read the message, he realized it was dangerously provocative. He sat up all evening carefully rewording it to take out the sting, and offering the United States government a way out by suggesting that the captain of the offending warship had exceeded his orders.

This perilous situation might have resulted in war, a war disastrous for Britain as well as the United States. But thanks to Albert's diplomacy, the temperature of the crisis dropped and the United States government accepted the terms of the British message. It was

95

fitting that Prince Albert's last act of statesmanship should have been a successful effort to preserve peace and friendship between his adopted country and its greatest future ally.

That night the prince lay shivering with cold. Sir James Clark, who had been court doctor during the Lady Flora Hastings affair twenty-two years before, still spoke of a "feverish sort of influenza." Sir James was now seventy-three, and in the opinion of Lord Clarendon, "not fit to attend a sick cat." Lord Palmerston, too, was worried and he insisted that a specialist be brought in.

The prince grew steadily worse, suffering bouts of delirium between his wanderings about the castle. The doctors at last admitted that he had "bowel fever," another name for typhoid. In trying not to alarm the queen, they made no proper arrangements for nursing the dangerous illness. Of course, by now the queen was terrified anyway.

The hours dragged by agonizingly as Victoria waited outside the door of Albert's room, tears streaming down her face. At last she heard him ask for his *Gütes Frauchen* ("dear little wife"). But to make the situation even harder for the queen, the dying man alternated between moods of affectionate gentleness and half-delirious rage, in which he relived old quarrels and shouted angrily at poor Victoria.

On Friday, December 13, the prince lay silent and

pale, his breath coming in shallow gasps and his mind wandering far away in his German homeland. The Prince of Wales was summoned from Cambridge, and the other children gathered nearby. At six o'clock the next morning, one of the doctors told Victoria he thought the crisis was over, but it was only the brief rallying that often precedes death.

All that day Albert lay quietly. The strain had gone from his face, and he looked once more like the handsome youth Victoria had greeted on the steps of Windsor Castle, so many years before. As life slipped away from him, his children, the doctors, and court officials gathered round the bed while Victoria sat holding his hand. Even at the last, the royal couple were not alone.

Throughout his illness Victoria had kept up the daily entries in her journal. Now there came a gap. More than ten years were to pass before she could steel herself to describe her husband's last hours.

Prince Albert died quietly, late in the evening of December 14. The queen leaned over and kissed his forehead at the last, then sank to her knees beside the bed, unmoving and unseeing. For a little while she could not even cry.

In the streets of London, people hurried home from theaters and parties in the dim yellow light of the gas lamps. Carriages trundled rapidly over the cobblestones, and a few gin-filled revelers tottered uneasily from the taverns. Suddenly all was still. The laughter and the conversation ceased, and people paused in a sort of dread, hearing a solemn sound. The great bell of Saint Paul's Cathedral was tolling the death of "Albert the Good."

CHAPTER VIII

Endurance

The death of Albert marked the end of one reign and the beginning of another: Victoria was to outlive him by forty years, nearly twice as long a time as their life together. During all that time the shadow of Albert's death hung over her. It plunged her from happiness into desolation, and for many months her only wish was that she might soon join him. Later, she told her children that she would go on living for their sake, and her actions would be guided entirely by what Albert would have wished.

The queen's personal tragedy also had a wider significance. Albert died in the prime of life at forty-two; had he lived another thirty years, the history of England, the British Empire, and the world might well have turned out differently.

Prime ministers come and go, but the monarch (or in Albert's case, the prince consort) remains. Only death removes him from office. Albert's knowledge, experience, and prestige, growing with the passing years, would doubtless have made him a figure of great influence in Britain. Through his ability and hard work, the monarchy had already become a more powerful institution; and an opponent as formidable as Lord Palmerston, in his conflict with the crown, had achieved nothing better than an honorable tie. Benjamin Disraeli went so far as to say that if the prince had lived he would have given England "the blessings of absolute government." Not everyone would have agreed that "absolute government" was much of a "blessing," and certainly Albert was not the kind of man to make himself a dictator. Nevertheless, he would surely have become a more powerful force in the British government.

Albert's death ended the possibility that the crown might again become a strong executive power. Victoria was not fitted, either by character, ability, or sex, to play so distinguished a part in politics. Previously, the crown had been represented by two people; now, it was reduced to one, and that one the weaker—a desperate, grief-stricken widow, who cried, "I depended on him body and soul."

At Christmastime, 1861, Victoria wrote to her uncle, King Leopold of the Belgians: "My *life* as a *happy* one is *ended*! the world is gone for *me*! . . . I had hoped with such instinctive certainty that God never *would* part us, and would let us grow old together (though *he* always talked of the shortness of life) [it] is *too awful,* too cruel!"

Dimly, behind her all too-genuine distress, one can sense a characteristic note of resentment that God had dared to strike her such a blow. Victoria's fighting spirit was not completely crushed. Nevertheless, her mourning for Albert was too intense and too prolonged. While she could not put an end to official business and was too dutiful to try, the bereaved queen refused to fulfill her equally important role of public figure. For several years her subjects never saw her. She would not open Parliament, visit exhibitions, name ships, or attend state functions. Her refusal to carry out the ceremonial side of her duties as sovereign provoked mounting criticism. Her popularity faded, and her continued seclusion from the world created, as will be seen, a number of awkward problems in the 1860's and 1870's.

The royal doctors were worried about the queen, for the death of Albert, following so closely upon the death of her mother, began to affect her physical and mental health. She welcomed the physicians' advice not to take part in public functions, but after two or three years of this, some people began to suspect that perhaps the doctors' orders were dictated to them by the royal patient herself.

Whenever a government minister or member of the

court tried to induce the queen to break out of her seclusion, Victoria became ill—or so it seemed. By 1869 there were many who shared Lord Clarendon's opinion that "Eliza [his irreverent name for the queen] is roaring well and can do everything she likes and nothing she doesn't." Others regarded her neurosis more seriously, for as Victoria herself often remarked in a meaningful way, her grandfather, George III, had gone mad.

Sometimes, though, the queen showed flashes of that solid common sense that was such an attractive feature of her character. Of a bishop's advice that she should now consider herself the wife of Christ, she later remarked: "That is what I call twaddle."

Although Queen Victoria undoubtedly overindulged her suffering, it would be hard to exaggerate the grief she endured in the early years of widowhood. Life seemed to hold nothing for her. Her children were only a slight comfort. Princess Alice and Princess Helena were her chief supports, and the baby of the family, Princess Beatrice, was a cheerful little creature who would clamber on the bed and prattle about "dear Papa." But Bertie, the Prince of Wales, made his mother shudder.

Victoria had got it into her head that Bertie's unfortunate "affair" had broken his father's heart and helped to cause his death. Not until the poor youth had taken a long trip abroad, in 1862, could she again treat him in a motherly way. The following year Bertie married the beautiful and charming Princess Alexandra of Denmark, who already had Victoria's warm approval, and from that time on, the queen's affection for her son and heir grew steadily warmer.

Despite the gloom that surrounded the court, Victoria did not think that death itself should be a gloomy affair. The mausoleum where Albert was finally laid to rest (with a place waiting by his side for her) gleamed with copper, mosaics, and white marble. It was not a somber place, but peaceful. Victoria would often go and sit there quietly.

Memorials to Albert appeared all over the country; even the place where he shot his last deer was marked by a statue. The lord mayor of London offered a site in Kensington for the capital's memorial, and Victoria's stipulation that it should be "of sufficient grandeur" was certainly obeyed. The prince, sculpted in marble, double life-size, sits today overlooking the Albert Hall. He holds a catalog of the Great Exhibition, and above him, a great canopy reaches toward the sky. Below stand groups of statues representing the arts and sciences, and wide, open steps lead down to the street. The style is Gothic with Oriental touches —an astounding example of Victorian panache that later generations found quite vulgar. As for Victoria, she thought it did not do its subject justice. Nothing, in her opinion, ever could.

Through the marriages of her numerous children, Queen Victoria was to become the matriarch of

European royalty. Already she had close relatives in nearly every reigning family. She sometimes tended to think of international relations as a family matter, and while this had some advantages, it also had drawbacks. The foreign policies of governments are not conducted for the convenience of royal relatives. Disputes between nations caused quarrels in the international royal family. The Schleswig-Holstein crisis was a case in point.

The politics of the Schleswig-Holstein question were very complicated indeed. Lord Palmerston hardly exaggerated when he said that only three people understood it: Prince Albert, and he was dead; a German professor, and he had gone mad; and himself, and he had forgotten all about it. Briefly, a long-standing dispute about who should have the twin duchies of Schleswig-Holstein came to a head in 1863 with the death of the king of Denmark. There were three claimants: the new king of Denmark, the duke of Augustenburg, and Prussia, where the great Otto von Bismarck had recently become chief minister.

Not only did this quarrel threaten to upset the peace of Europe, but it also split Victoria's family into conflicting factions. Her eldest son was married to the king of Denmark's daughter; her niece was married to the duke of Augustenburg; and her eldest daughter was married to the crown prince of Prussia. Thus the poor queen was bombarded with opposing views, for naturally her son supported Denmark while her daughter wrote angry letters on behalf of Prussia.

Victoria's own views were dictated by what she believed Albert would have wished, and that meant guarded support for the Germans (Prussia). For once the queen's opinion differed from the majority of the British people, who sympathized with Denmark. When Prussia, in alliance with Austria, invaded the duchies and defeated the Danish army, many people in Britain believed that they ought to be fighting on the Danish side. But France refused to join with the British, and Lord Palmerston would not go to war in such dangerous circumstances. Nobody, not even Bismarck himself, realized that this was the first step toward the creation of a Prussian-dominated German empire.

The Schleswig-Holstein crisis taught Victoria several lessons, some of them valuable, some dangerous. She had been drawn into the thick of foreign policy for the first time since Albert's death, and this reinforced her conviction that she had a special mission in foreign affairs. Later ministers, Gladstone particularly, were to find that conviction extremely inconvenient. On the other hand, the queen learned that she was not completely helpless without Albert's guidance. At one point during the crisis, she actually recorded her relief that Albert had been spared all the worry, "for he could have done even less than I can."

Victoria sometimes said how much she disliked

being queen. After Albert's death it seemed impossible to go on, and she hoped and believed that she too would soon be dead so that they might be together again. Although she was sincere, this was not the whole truth. She could, for instance, have abdicated the hated crown in favor of the Prince of Wales, who was older than she herself had been when she came to the throne. In fact, many people expected her to do so. Yet she never considered it. Perhaps she thought that Bertie was not fit to reign, but if she had died as she expected, he would have been king anyway. Her instinct for self-preservation was stronger than she realized, and her liking for power was greater than she could admit, even to herself. As many writers have said, it is the contradictions in Queen Victoria's character that make her so interesting as a person.

In the Schleswig-Holstein crisis she showed a firm grasp of events and battled with Lord Palmerston as vigorously as ever when she disagreed with him. But she still remained in deep seclusion, giving ill health as the reason.

After two years, sympathy for the queen's bereavement had worn thin. The *Times* of London was severe in its criticism, and Victoria, rather surprisingly, sent a letter to the editor defending her conduct in forthright terms. The letter was unsigned, but its vigorous style betrayed its authorship. It did not stop the criticism, however. In March, 1864, some prankster stuck a notice on the railings at Buckingham Palace:

"These commanding premises to be let or sold, in consequence of the late occupant's declining business." The queen was not amused.

While Victoria clung to her grief as though she did not want to recover from it, healing time was doing its work in spite of her. A note of resignation in her letters gradually replaced the cries of anguish, and she began to feel that her life still had an aim and a purpose: "I must endure as long as God wills it," she wrote in May, 1865, "and when I know and feel that I can promote good, maintain order, prevent evil and advance the general welfare; then I am prepared to continue so long as my weak and shattered nerves endure." She would have been surprised to learn that her "weak and shattered nerves" were to endure for thirty-six more years.

The brevity of life was brought home to her again in 1865 with the deaths of two people she connected with the happy past. Lord Palmerston, who had begun to seem immortal, especially to his political opponents, passed from the scene in October. "He had many valuable qualities," Queen Victoria wrote, "though many bad ones." On the whole, she thought, "he is a great loss."

A sadder loss, two months later, was King Leopold of the Belgians, at the age of seventy-five. "That dear loving Uncle, who has ever been to me as a Father," Victoria described him in her journal. How she would miss his wise and affectionate letters. Leopold was her last real link with her own childhood. Now there was nobody left, she complained pathetically, who could call her Victoria.

Loneliness is one of the penalties of eminence. The queen had no really close friends and no relatives near her, except her children. They were very good, she said, but naturally they put their own families first (four were now married). Only Baby Beatrice, and perhaps Princess Helena, loved her more than anyone else.

More and more her ladies-in-waiting tended to be widows like herself, and when one of them married a second time, the queen was furious. Victoria seemed to feel that widowhood was a holy state, and she was always deeply sympathetic toward anyone who lost a wife or a husband. When the American President Lincoln was assassinated, she hastened to write a letter to his widow that was touching, though quaint: "Dear Madam,—Though a stranger to you, I cannot remain silent when so terrible a calamity has fallen upon you and your country..."

In February, 1866, the queen at last agreed to open Parliament in person, although the ceremony was shortened at her insistence. She was driven through large crowds of curious, rather silent onlookers, and afterward she felt exhausted and faint. Still, Victoria got through it, and Princess Helena thought she seemed calmer and happier once the trying function was over.

Toward the end of that year an unexpected sympathizer appeared in the person of John Bright, the famous spokesman of the radical wing of the Liberal party, who was no admirer of the institution of monarchy. Bright told his surprised audience that "there has been, by many persons, a great injustice done to the Queen in reference to her desolate and widowed position. And I venture to say this, that a woman—be she queen of a great realm, or be she the wife of one of your labouring men—who can keep alive in her heart a great sorrow for the lost object of her life and affection, is not at all likely to be wanting in a great and generous sympathy with you."

Meanwhile, on the Continent, Bismarck's policy of "blood and iron" again brought strife to Europe and to the queen's family circle. Having used Austria to help take Schleswig-Holstein from the Danes, Bismarck now turned against his former ally and manufactured a quarrel to precipitate war. Once more, Victoria's children were on different sides. Despite the impassioned plea she sent to the king of Prussia, who, she said, was "deceived . . . [by] *one* man" (i.e., Bismarck), the armies of Prussia and Austria clashed. The Austrians were routed, and the war ended only seven weeks after it began, with Prussian domination of Germany fully confirmed.

CHAPTER IX

"*Wumman*" and "*Faery*"

During her long reign a succession of interesting men moved through Victoria's life. The four men whom the queen, in quite different ways, loved best were: her husband, Prince Albert; two prime ministers, Melbourne and Disraeli; and a Scottish servant, John Brown.

Brown was picked out by Prince Albert as the most reliable of the Scottish servants who attended the royal family at Balmoral. He used to lead the queen's pony on rides through the hills, and his fondness for his country's most famous product, Scotch whisky, never seemed to interfere with his duties.

After Albert's death, the queen's doctors wanted her to exercise, but she would not take a step out of doors. Someone suggested getting Brown to bring her favorite pony down from Scotland, and Victoria agreed. Late in 1864, Brown became the queen's personal servant, and from that time on his career blossomed. The menial tasks that he had been appointed to carry out, such as cleaning boots or looking after the royal dogs, were soon reassigned to humbler folk. Brown was fully occupied in his attendance on the queen, and—to the great astonishment of her correspondents—the queen soon began to quote Brown's opinions in her letters.

Victoria found that Brown was "a *real* comfort, for he is *so* devoted to me—so simple, so intelligent, *so unlike* an *ordinary* servant, and so cheerful and attentive. . . ." By 1872 she was writing to Brown himself that she was anxious to show how much he meant to her. "Every one hears me say you are *my friend* & most confidential attendant." Everyone did hear it, but nobody was pleased about it.

No doubt Brown was good for Victoria and helped her get over the grief of Albert's death. With his bushy beard and his swirling kilt, he was an impressive figure—handsome, strong, and gruff. He sometimes treated the queen as if she were an idle maidservant, and she, secure in the knowledge of his honesty and devotion, merely smiled tolerantly. Lords and prime ministers wrote to her in the formal third person and never called her by a less exalted title than "Your Majesty." Brown, pinning up her cloak at the neck one day, was heard to say, "Can ye no hold your head up, wumman?"

"WUMMAN" AND "FAERY"

But a reigning queen, as Victoria herself often admitted, cannot pick her friends freely. Brown's privileged position caused a succession of fierce rows. That feature of his character that the queen especially admired—his outspoken honesty—was not well suited to life at court. He often delivered the queen's messages in his own shortened form which showed, to say the least, a want of tact. One day in 1869 the mayor of Portsmouth was at Osborne, waiting for a reply to his official request that the queen should attend some civic function in his city. The door burst open and in strode Brown. "The Queen says certainly not!" he announced. The mayor went away fuming.

The court soon began grumbling about Brown's presumptuous behavior. The Prince of Wales and all of the queen's children disliked him, and occasional attempts were made to persuade Victoria to give him up. This required boldness, for the least whisper against Brown often provoked an outburst of regal wrath.

If it had been only her family and courtiers who resented Brown, no great harm would have been done; but, unfortunately, the peculiar relationship between the queen and her servant soon became a matter of public gossip. An American visitor to London was appalled by the stories he heard from quite respectable people: that the queen had secretly married Brown; that she was insane and Brown was her medical attendant; that she believed in spirits and Brown was the medium through whom she communicated with Prince Albert; and a hundred other stories, "each more absurd than the other."

Jokes about "Mrs. Brown" kept the popular press busy for years. Cartoons and satirical articles made the most of the scandal, and the newspapers of foreign countries, including the United States, sometimes joined in.

The nastiest rumors never reached Victoria's ears. And nothing could make her give up "good Brown." To her, his strength was a comfort and a reassurance, and more than once he saved her from a severe accident when out driving (horse-drawn carriages were no less accident-prone than present-day automobiles, and Victoria's was overturned at least a dozen times). Once, when a madman tried to shoot her, Brown was the one who grabbed the assailant's pistol.

The unfortunate public scandal was largely the result of Victoria's seclusion. Her subjects never saw her and not seeing her, they imagined the worst. In the 1870's, when she began to appear more often, the gossip died down, and by the time Brown died in 1883, the scandal had long been forgotten.

Actually, Brown was merely the outstanding symbol and beneficiary of Queen Victoria's partiality for the humbler classes of her subjects, especially the Scottish cottagers. There was no shadow of truth in the suspicion that Brown was her lover, and everybody who knew the queen regarded such a suggestion as utterly absurd.

The other great friend of Victoria's middle age was a very different man. While his status was more orthodox than John Brown's, his character was far more unusual. He was Benjamin Disraeli, who first became Conservative prime minister in 1868. Disraeli was a man of many talents and of powerful ambition. Descended from an immigrant Italian Jew, he had never been to college and had no connection with the landowning aristocracy of the Conservative party. Moreover, he was the author of several rather scandalous novels. A less likely man to be a Conservative prime minister could hardly be imagined. Disraeli had "climbed to the top of the greasy pole" (as he described his success in politics) by his ability, courage, and hard work.

Earlier, when his name was first put forward as a potential minister in the brief Conservative government of 1852, Queen Victoria had not been pleased: "I do not approve of Mr. D. I do not approve of his conduct to Sir Robert Peel." For it was Disraeli who had led the Conservative rebels in the Corn Laws crisis that brought down Peel's government in 1846. Nevertheless, Victoria agreed to accept him. Disraeli soon aroused the queen's interest by his "curious" reports of debates in Parliament. Soon afterward, Disraeli and his wife received an invitation to dine.

Benjamin Disraeli, British statesman and author, who later was created Lord Beaconsfield. His considerable wit and charm made him Queen Victoria's favorite prime minister. (Charles Phelps Cushing)

The queen recorded her impression: "[He] is most singular—thoroughly Jewish looking, a livid complexion, dark eyes & eyebrows & black ringlets. . . . He has a very bland manner, & his language is very flowery." Clearly the queen, though intrigued, was not yet captivated.

After the death of Prince Albert, Disraeli's "bland manner" and "flowery language" had been usefully employed in the letter he wrote the queen: "The Prince is the only person whom Mr. Disraeli has ever known who realised the Ideal. . . . There was in him a union of the manly grace and sublime simplicity, of chivalry with the intellectual splendour of the Attic Academe." And Disraeli had written much more in the same vein.

This exalted opinion exactly fitted Victoria's own. Nobody else, she thought, had described Albert's virtues as perfectly as Mr. Disraeli. She rewarded him with a copy of the prince's speeches bound in white, which drew another paean of praise from Disraeli's smooth pen. The queen gradually forgot that she had once disliked him; she forgot that Prince Albert had said Disraeli was not a gentleman and lacked principles. In time, his extravagant devotion to herself and his undeniable charm (which enchanted other middle-aged ladies besides herself) made him Victoria's favorite prime minister, eclipsing even Lord Melbourne.

It was much easier to conduct the business of the

country with the friendly support of the queen. William Gladstone, Disraeli's great rival, was to find how difficult the job of prime minister could be when the queen was an opponent. Many people supposed that Disraeli set out deliberately to flatter the queen's vanity with his fulsome compliments and constant expressions of devotion, and "Dizzy," as everyone called him, supplied much of the evidence for this charge. "Everyone likes flattery," he once said, "and when you come to royalty you should lay it on with a trowel."

But although Disraeli was a shrewd and practical politician and a rather cynical wit, he was at heart a romantic. The whole aura of royalty fascinated him; he admired all the great traditional institutions of England—crown, church, and Parliament—and he responded enthusiastically to the glories of their history. The desire to do great things spurred his ambition; life was a game which should be played with grace and boldness.

Both as a sovereign and as a woman, Queen Victoria appealed to Disraeli's imagination. (He never forgot that she was both.) He called her "the Faery," an allusion to Edmund Spenser's famous poem *The Faery Queene* about Queen Elizabeth I, and despite the touch of irony in the epithet, Disraeli really did regard the plump little lady in black as a creature of grandeur and romance.

As she grew older, Victoria became more obstinate

and, at times, more self-centered. When her wishes conflicted with her ministers' plans, trouble loomed. Disraeli himself sometimes had to retreat, but on the whole he handled her successfully. He was always careful to ask her advice, though he sometimes "forgot" to act on it. He spoke of her great wisdom and experience and his own ignorance and feebleness; but on important matters he made sure that he, not the queen, made the decisions.

Victoria always thought of herself as a Liberal, but as time passed she became increasingly conservative. Personalities often meant more to her than policies, and her devotion to Disraeli helped to make her a Conservative supporter, while her loathing for Gladstone helped to make her an anti-Liberal. Gladstone seemed to her a dangerous revolutionary, yet Disraeli had no difficulty in persuading her that his famous Reform Act of 1867, which was as "revolutionary" as any act of Gladstone's, was both necessary and desirable.

As a young woman, Victoria had been afraid of intellectual people, because they made her feel ignorant. Yet Albert's influence and the passing years had cured her feelings of inferiority. She told her eldest daughter, in 1863, that she felt a need to have clever men around her. Accordingly, Victoria met most of the literary giants of the age during the 1860's. At the house of one of her ladies-in-waiting she was introduced to the philosopher Thomas Carlyle (who, she thought, was rather gloomy), to J. A. Froude the historian, and to the poet Robert Browning. The poet laureate, Alfred, Lord Tennyson, had the advantage of Albert's approval, and he became a close friend. Sometimes the queen asked him to read his poems to her.

Charles Dickens was also among the favored few who were honored with an invitation to Buckingham Palace. The greatest novelist of the age told the queen that he thought divisions of social class would one day disappear. Victoria, who was no snob (except about royalty), answered that she earnestly hoped he was right.

In 1868 the queen herself became an author with the publication of *Leaves from the Journal of Our Life in the Highlands*. It was a simple account of life at Balmoral, with no excitement and no drama, but including some amiable gossip about the servants, which courtiers thought very unwise. Though the volume was expensive, it sold out at once. This success the queen attributed to the picture it gave of modest family life, which she hoped would set an example to "highborn beings"—those dissolute people of fashionable society whom the Prince of Wales, alas, was so friendly with. More likely, it was the name of the author which chiefly accounted for the sales.

After this satisfying little accomplishment, Victoria

began to think that she, too, was something of a literary person. Benjamin Disraeli, author of numerous very successful novels and other books, perhaps encouraged her by sometimes speaking of "We authors, Ma'am," at which she smiled, but, all the same, felt a glow of pride.

The queen's writing style was certainly an individual one, although in *Leaves from the Journal* she was more restrained than she was in her diary and in her letters. Her style cannot be called good: it was full of clichés, bad grammar, and words used in the wrong sense. Nevertheless, it was extremely vivid and highly expressive of her personality. These literary virtues were perhaps greater than her faults. If she had been born in a comfortable middle-class home, it is possible to imagine her becoming a popular lady novelist—a breed that flourished in this period. For Victoria had plenty of imagination and she wrote quickly and easily, as the enormous quantity of her correspondence shows. She read novels with enjoyment, including Disraeli's, but later in life, when she grew more prudish, she found many books too "coarse." She was not an intellectual, and she could not maintain Albert's standards of serious reading. She once told C. L. Dodgson (Lewis Carroll), who besides being the author of wonderful fairy stories was also a mathematics professor, that she had greatly admired his *Alice in Wonderland*. He promptly sent her a copy of his next book, which was entitled *Syllabus of Plane Algebraical Geometry*. The queen, very sensibly, did not read it.

Family affairs helped to bring the queen gradually out of her retirement. Her children's marriages and the birth of grandchildren helped keep her occupied. Whenever possible, she liked to be with her married daughters for the birth of her grandchildren, and she was full of advice on every possible subject, from baby food to court etiquette. By now the queen was the head of a very large family, and as they multiplied and she grew older, her stature as the mother figure of European royalty became more and more impressive.

Victoria was finding self-confidence. Insecure as a child, later protected by an adoring husband, and then devastated by his death, she had never felt sure of her own judgment. Now that it had become necessary to stand on her own feet she found she could do it quite easily. When Albert was alive she had made no decisions without his advice; he had even chosen her bonnets for her. By 1870 she was beginning to feel that her opinions were probably more accurate than anyone else's, and she was at last beginning to realize that life went on—the world had not ended with Albert's death. And, though Albert was never wrong, of course, his ideas could no longer be applied in every situation.

Visits of foreign royalty forced the queen to appear at state functions, and while she protested, she was

Queen Victoria as she appeared in the late 1860s. After the death of Prince Albert, she was often referred to as "the Widow of Windsor," due to the black bonnet she wore in almost constant bereavement. (Charles Phelps Cushing)

privately rather pleased by the great reception held for the sultan of Turkey in 1867. As usual, moments of farce threatened to disrupt the solemnities. The sultan had expressed his interest in the navy, and it was therefore decided to award him the Order of the Garter aboard ship. Unfortunately the day was stormy, and the ceremony was interrupted several times as the seasick sultan suddenly had to rush below.

When the queen learned that she would have to postpone her departure to Balmoral for three days owing to the sultan's visit, she was most displeased. Out came the old arguments: she could not be expected, alone and feeble as she was, to make these sacrifices for reasons of state. Nobody dared suggest that a three-day postponement of her vacation was not such a great sacrifice, but it was tactfully pointed out that to leave the capital in the middle of the state visit of the ruler of a foreign power might be regarded as downright insulting. The queen, though still grumbling, agreed to stay.

Even devoted courtiers who had known and loved her for thirty years sometimes found Victoria a difficult mistress. Everyone was a little afraid of her. When displeased, she could be quite terrifying. Her mouth would go down at the corners and her large eyes would bulge with a cold glare. No one could administer a more devastating snub than Queen Victoria. Once when she was opening a public library, the librarian, making the most of his moment in the limelight, pushed his daughter forward to introduce her to the queen. "I came to see the Library," Her Majesty said stonily, ignoring them both.

But Victoria was seldom unreasonable. A little gentleness, a little tact, even a little romance—this was the mixture to melt her obstinacy. Disraeli employed such tactics with notable success. It was a pity that others could not imitate his talent for drawing out the fundamental warmth and goodwill of the lonely queen.

Disraeli had shown brilliant mastery of Parliament in gaining approval for the Reform Act of 1867, but his wizardry could not sustain the weak Conservative government for long. In the hope of increasing the number of Conservatives, a parliamentary election was held late in 1868. The result was a decisive victory for the Liberal party under its new leader, William Gladstone.

On December 3, Gladstone went to Windsor for the first time as prime minister. "Nothing could be more satisfactory than the whole interview," the queen noted. It was almost the only satisfactory interview with Mr. Gladstone that she ever had.

CHAPTER X

Liberalism

The confusion of British politics since 1846 came to an end with the Liberal victory in the parliamentary election of 1868. From then on, two roughly equal parties, Liberals and Conservatives, shared power between them. The numerous minor divisions of the earlier period ceased to be important, and, as the chorus sang in Gilbert and Sullivan's *Iolanthe*:

> ... every boy and every girl
> That's born into this world alive
> Is either a little Liberal
> Or else a little Conservative.

Party leadership was also more stable. Disraeli and his successor, Lord Salisbury, headed the Conservative party for the rest of the reign, and from 1868 to 1894 William Ewart Gladstone led the Liberals.

When people talk about "eminent Victorians" (the title of a famous book by Lytton Strachey) or "great Victorians," Gladstone is usually the first name that springs to mind. He had many of the characteristics most often associated with the age—energy, the will to succeed, piety, a belief in the moral value of hard work and prayer, and honesty that was sometimes spoiled by narrow-mindedness—but in him every quality seemed exaggerated. Although he was not particularly tall, everything about Gladstone appeared bigger than normal, including his collars (to the delight of cartoonists). The greatest British politician of the century, he loomed over his contemporaries like a giant among pygmies.

Conservative supporters might claim that title for their hero, Benjamin Disraeli, and it was an odd stroke of fate that brought two such brilliant men into conflict. Utterly different in every way, they waged their war of words throughout the mid-Victorian period, when the mother of Parliaments reached the height of its prestige. Such a clash of titans has not been seen in the House of Commons before or since.

Gladstone always declared, quite sincerely, that he had no ambition. What drove him on with such unflagging determination—so he believed—was the will of God. Although he changed his mind on many important issues during his long career, he was always completely convinced of the rightness of his own opinions. Gladstone's moral fervor did not easily tolerate opposition: he could never believe that Disraeli, or any other opponent, might be as sincere as he himself was. This was the reason for Palmerston's remark, years before, that Gladstone was "a dangerous man."

It was a Liberal supporter, on the occasion of Gladstone's sudden adoption of an unexpected policy, who commented that he did not mind Gladstone's habit of suddenly producing the ace of trumps from up his sleeve, but he did object to his assumption that it was put there by God.

Prince Albert had thought well of Gladstone, and Victoria had, at first, echoed his opinion. In the 1860's, however, she was irritated by Gladstone's opposition to the Conservatives and by what she regarded as his "inflammatory" speeches in favor of reform. His vote against the Albert Memorial in Kensington in 1863 had annoyed her extremely, and when he became prime minister in 1868 she was less than enthusiastic, especially as he was replacing Disraeli. But as the comment in her journal shows, no sign of hostility marked Gladstone's first interview.

Unfortunately, their relationship soon began to deteriorate, and it continued to do so throughout their long association (Gladstone was prime minister for a total of thirteen years between 1868 and 1894).

Unlike Disraeli, Gladstone had no notion of how to handle the queen. "Dizzy" would send her brief and witty summaries of parliamentary debates, but

Mr. Gladstone inundated her with vast essays arranged under numbered subheadings and composed in the most obscure prose. While Disraeli charmed, Gladstone pontificated. Disraeli always remembered that the queen was a woman; Gladstone treated her as an institution. He tended to lecture her as if she were a public meeting, and his well-meant attempts to explain his policy in detail left the queen bewildered and irritated. Victoria said she "always felt in his manner an overbearing obstinacy and imperiousness . . . which she never experienced from *anyone* else, and which she found most disagreeable." Mrs. Gladstone, a better psychologist than her husband, advised him to "pet" the queen. But Gladstone was incapable of insincerity, and to him Victoria was the sovereign, the crown, the head of state—not a pet.

If Gladstone failed to understand the queen, the queen equally failed to understand Gladstone: she could not follow the sometimes complicated reasons for his actions. Gladstone once resigned from a government in which he was a minister over a policy which, though he agreed with it, he had once, years before, opposed. His action was dictated by conscience, but the queen thought it at best silly and at worst sinister. If he agreed, why resign? she asked.

Victoria was not the only person who found the workings of Gladstone's conscience inexplicable, and those who could not understand him naturally distrusted him, although Victoria acknowledged that he

A portrait of William Ewart Gladstone. He was prime minister four times during Queen Victoria's reign. (Charles Phelps Cushing)

was loyal to her personally. His attempts to persuade her to leave her retirement, which, like everything else, he urged too violently, she interpreted as an attempt to win public support for the Liberal party. In fact, Gladstone was thinking of the benefit to the country as a whole.

While the queen could not bring herself to like Gladstone as a person, she would not have objected to him as strongly if she had agreed with his politics. Far from agreeing, she thought Gladstone's political views were dangerous, wrong, and bad for the country. As sovereign, she was bound to support the British government, but she found it increasingly hard to support a government which she believed was thoroughly misguided.

Gladstone had started his political career as a Conservative. Like his chief, Sir Robert Peel, he was gradually converted to Liberalism, but he went much further than Peel and became, in effect, the founder of the British Liberal party. As had Palmerston, he supported nationalism in Italy against the Austrian Empire, but unlike Palmerston, he did not believe in the aggressive assertion of British interests in Europe. Rather, he hoped to reduce expenditure on defense and keep clear of foreign quarrels.

At home, Gladstone generally supported political reform, and though he respected the old institutions of Britain, he was not afraid of change. When Gladstone believed that change was necessary, no power on earth could stop him from straining every nerve to achieve it.

Gladstone's intense religious feeling was characteristic of his age. Worldly people like Lord Melbourne might question the existence of God, but they generally kept their doubts to themselves, and as the century wore on, religion became more and more a subject of intense and deeply felt argument.

England was of course, a Protestant country, and it had (and still has) an "established" church. The Church of England is recognized by the state as the national religious institution, and it therefore enjoys all kinds of privileges, particularly financial and social. In Victorian times, someone who was not a member of the Church of England could not hold certain offices. Thus Disraeli, had he retained the Jewish faith of his ancestors, could never have sat in Parliament.

While there was strong opposition to the Church of England from the growing number of "Dissenters" (Methodists, Presbyterians, and others), the majority of the population belonged to the Church of England and were perfectly satisfied with it. However, this was not the case in Ireland, where the established Protestant church was supported by the taxes of a population that was mainly Roman Catholic.

It is strange that nineteenth-century Englishmen believed so firmly that they were fit to govern other peoples on distant continents when they failed to govern successfully a country that lay on their very doorstep. Throughout this period Ireland was poor, sometimes starving, exploited, and, not surprisingly, rebellious. Hatred of England was widespread, and many people emigrated to the United States. There some of them founded the movement known as Fenianism, dedicated to the destruction of British rule in Ireland. Gladstone was to devote his greatest efforts to solving the Irish problem; but he was to fail.

Irish Roman Catholics resented having to support a Protestant church when their own religion received no support at all. Most reasonable Englishmen acknowledged the injustice of this situation, and a movement to "disestablish" the Irish Protestant church gathered strength in the 1860's. Disraeli, faced with this movement, nevertheless decided against disestablishment, not because he approved of the oppression of Roman Catholics in Ireland but because he (and many others) feared that to disestablish the Irish church would create a precedent dangerous to the Church of England itself. So strong was the pressure for disestablishment in Ireland that Disraeli was forced to submit his policy to the people in the parliamentary election of 1868. That was the election that brought Gladstone and the Liberals to power.

Earlier in his career, Gladstone had supported the Protestant church in Ireland, but now, as leader of the recent opposition to Disraeli, he was determined to end its privileged position. All of Gladstone's powers of oratory were invoked to convince Parliament of his view, and as the Liberals had a large majority in the House of Commons, the outcome was never seriously in doubt. The House of Lords, as always, was more Conservative, but it was still dangerous for the Lords to obstruct the policy of the government. The Lords held their seats by right of inheritance, and if they opposed the Commons, whose members were the *elected* representatives of the people, they provoked the hostile cry of "aristocratic government," accompanied by threats to reform or abolish the House of Lords.

Over the disestablishment bill, however, the Conservative Lords seemed to be willing to take the risk of incurring the wrath of the Commons. The queen recognized the danger to the constitution if the Lords and Commons clashed head on, and not for the first or the last time she stepped in as peacemaker.

Victoria hated the bill no less than the Conservative Lords. As monarch, she was also head of the established church, and Gladstone's blow at the church was, indirectly, a blow at her. She had begun by suggesting to the Lords that they should try to amend the bill to make it less effective. But when she saw that a major crisis was blowing up, she wisely retreated from this provocative (and unconstitional) suggestion. A fight between Lords and Commons would be even more dangerous, she realized, than Irish disestablishment. Hastily recollecting that her duty was to support the government, she persuaded the Lords to withdraw their opposition.

However, she refused to perform the ceremony of opening Parliament in person for "reasons of health," which angered Gladstone because she had been well enough to open it for Disraeli when the Conservatives were in power.

Having settled the problem of the Irish church, Gladstone turned to the graver problem of the rent and ownership of land in Ireland. The desperately poor Irish peasants rented small plots of land, often in return for their labor. As land was scarce and labor plentiful, these people were in a poor position to bargain with the landlord—or rather, the landlord's agent, for the absentee owner himself often lived in luxury in England or elsewhere. They had no security, and a landlord could, and often did, throw the peasant out whenever it suited him. The law therefore favored the landlord, and the only weapon the peasants had was violence and terrorism. As a result, Ireland was constantly on the brink of anarchy.

The British government failed to deal with this problem except by force, partly because Englishmen never fully understood Irish conditions, and partly because the complete overhaul that was required would have been extremely expensive. (Yet the British government had paid over $100,000,000 in compensation to slave owners when it abolished slavery, and most of the Irish peasants were no better off than slaves.) The failure to deal with the Irish land problem was a grave charge against successive British governments in the nineteenth century.

But Gladstone at least tried. "My mission is to pacify Ireland," he had said when he became prime minister. His Irish land act of 1870, in fact, met with very little opposition in the British Parliament, but that was because the act was merely a moderate reform: it did not attack the root of the problem. It provided for compensation to tenants who had been evicted, but it failed to prevent landlords from raising rents beyond the ability of their tenants to pay. In any case, the time was perhaps already past when Ireland could be pacified by reforms introduced through the hated British government. Later, Gladstone himself was to recognize this.

Queen Victoria must, in retrospect, share the blame for the callous and shortsighted English treatment of Ireland. In her reign of sixty-four years she spent just one month in that desperate country, and she refused to allow the Prince of Wales to live there as viceroy, a sensible plan that Disraeli tactfully mentioned and Gladstone endlessly urged. In reality, Victoria did not like the Irish. Lord Melbourne had told her they were "troublesome," and the many stories of assassinations, secret societies, and terrorism convinced her that he was right. Her fear of revolution was stronger than her sympathy for impoverished peasants, and rumors of Fenian plots against her life, though she thought they were exaggerated, did not endear the Irish to her.

There was, perhaps, another reason for her hostility toward Ireland. The queen had given her heart to Scotland, to its craggy hills and simple people. Ireland had rather similar characteristics, and Victoria possibly felt jealous of Ireland as a rival to her beloved Scotland. One of her favorite ladies at court, Lady Augusta Stanley, once remarked that the queen was afraid that Ireland might "throw Balmoral into the shade."

On the continent of Europe, Prussia continued to "swallow up everything," as the queen disapprovingly put it. Chancellor Bismarck reworded the famous "Ems telegram" from the Prussian king to the French emperor to make the message sound insulting, and so provoked France into a declaration of war in 1870.

As usual, a European war meant war among Victoria's relatives. Gladstone's carefully neutral foreign policy reduced her effectiveness as a peacemaker, and her pro-German feelings were resented by the British people.

The Franco-Prussian War was short and decisive. The French were defeated, and the French provinces of Alsace and Lorraine became part of the German Empire which, engineered by Bismarck, came into being in 1871.

In France, defeat was followed by a coup in which the emperor was overthrown and a republic declared. This event encouraged republicans throughout Europe, including Britain. The queen, who had already lost respect by her seclusion and her pro-German sympathies, found herself again the object of attack. To make matters worse, the Prince of Wales had recently been involved in another scandal, and though he was innocent of every crime except foolishness, the affair had not made the monarchy any more popular with the increasingly puritanical middle classes.

Sir Charles Dilke, a Radical member of Parliament, attacked the monarchy in a public meeting in Newcastle. Another member of Parliament wrote an article, "What Does She Do With It?"—"it" being the very large royal income. The answer, he suggested, was that she was hoarding it away like a miser. Victoria urged Mr. Gladstone to condemn such talk, but though Gladstone had not a shred of sympathy with republicanism, his condemnation of Dilke and others was not, in the queen's view, sufficiently strong.

In the fall of 1871, Victoria was very ill with an abscess on her arm. As usual, the royal doctors showed very little ability at effecting a cure. For some months the queen really was unable to undertake public tasks, but the cry of "Wolf" had been heard so often that people believed this illness, too, was a sham.

Hardly had she recovered when the Prince of Wales

came down with the dreaded typhoid fever. The doctors almost despaired of Bertie's life, but on December 14, the anniversary of his father's death from the same disease, he began to improve. A service of thanksgiving for his recovery was later held in Saint Paul's Cathedral. The queen drove to the cathedral in an open carriage and during the service she electrified the congregation by dramatically clasping her son's hand and pressing it to her lips. It was a rare display of royal emotion in public.

Two days later, another incompetent assassin (an Irishman) attempted to bring the reign to a violent and sudden end, but he was quickly seized by John Brown.

These misfortunes—the prince's illness and Victoria's narrow escape—had the usual effect on public opinion. People who had been grumbling about the monarchy a few weeks before forgot all their complaints in sympathy for the queen. When Sir Charles Dilke renewed his attack on the monarchy in Parliament, hisses and jeers drowned his speech.

Meanwhile, the Franco-Prussian War had completely altered the balance of power in Europe. Germany was suddenly a very formidable state while France, for the time being, could be counted out. France's weakness emboldened Russia to question the settlement of the Turkish question made after the Crimean War. Britain protested, but without France she could offer no serious resistance. With Bismarck acting as mediator, a compromise was worked out, but people in Britain began to grumble that Gladstone's government was squandering Britain's international prestige. This opinion was strengthened by the settlement of the *Alabama* claims in 1872, though in this case Gladstone could hardly be blamed.

During the American Civil War, the Confederate States commissioned the construction of two ships in a British port. This was illegal, but it was difficult to prove that the ships were going to be used in warfare. The first ship was completed and it sailed for its destination in the South, but the Union's able minister in London, Charles Francis Adams, obtained a legal injunction to prevent the second ship, the *Alabama*, from sailing. However, the *Alabama* ignored the injunction and made its getaway while on a supposed trial cruise. During the next two years this powerful ironclad vessel sank and damaged many Union ships.

After the war, the United States government presented Britain with a bill for the damage caused by the notorious *Alabama*, but Britain rejected it. Eventually, the argument was submitted to an international court, which decided in 1872 that the United States was in the right. Gladstone's government then handed over the enormous sum of $15,000,000, which even the United States government thought was generous. In England, payment of so large a sum was taken as a spineless surrender to the Americans.

The early momentum of the Liberal government

had faded. Gladstone's great reform movements had made many enemies, and he himself spoke of retiring from politics (he was now over sixty). Two of his colleagues had been accused of graft. Disraeli, from his seat in the House of Commons, compared the Liberal ministers on the bench opposite with a range of extinct volcanoes.

In the parliamentary election of 1874, the first election in which—thanks to one of Gladstone's reforms—the vote was secret, the Liberals were defeated. For the first time since the fall of Sir Robert Peel in 1846, the Conservatives gained an overall majority in the House of Commons. The irrepressible "Dizzy," now seventy but still in full possession of his old wizardry and charm, received the queen's summons to form a government. Victoria heaved a sigh of relief as Mr. Gladstone gloomily departed for, he said, retirement. She could not quite believe she had seen the last of him. Nor had she.

CHAPTER XI

The British Empire

In the nineteenth century, Britain became for a short time the most powerful country in the world: British influence, British products, and British arms spanned the continents. A glance at a map of the world in about 1890 shows the vast extent of British possessions; for, measured in square miles, the British Empire was the greatest that has ever existed. It was an empire on which, as Rudyard Kipling wrote, "the sun never set."

The possession of such an empire made Great Britain neither as rich nor as powerful as the map suggests. Despite the dominance of the British navy, communications were an enormous problem; administration could never be truly efficient, and most of the colonies cost Britain more than they earned. The empire, or most of it, had been acquired in a haphazard, almost accidental manner. With some exceptions, Britain did not set out to acquire land as colonies. The motive behind imperialism was, to start with, an economic one. Britain thrived on commerce and industry, and in seeking new sources of trade and raw materials, she became involved in the political or economic organization of new lands. In such places the British often found themselves reluctantly drawn into the task of administration and government. They were not merely gun-toting exploiters of innocent peoples. They were often stupid and they were sometimes cruel, but they were not hypocritical villains, greedy for conquest.

There were really two British empires. The "old" empire was based on the lands called Dominions—Canada, Australia, and New Zealand—which had been acquired during the eighteenth century. The second empire had India as its cornerstone, but achieved its most rapid growth during the 1880's, when all the major European countries took part in the so-called scramble for colonies in Africa.

It was not until the early years of Victoria's reign that people began to think seriously about colonies. Although Britain had possessed them for well over two hundred years, no constructive plans had been made for their development. Many English people thought they were nothing more than a nuisance, and that their only advantages were that they might provide a safety valve for the expanding British population, a future market for British products, and a source of valuable minerals.

In the 1830's the colonial system came under more serious scrutiny and discussion. New questions about colonies were asked. Should the far-flung possessions of Britain be governed by a few uninterested officials in some poky government office? Or should the colonies be encouraged to develop systematically, adopting the institutions of the mother country? In particular, should not a legislature, like the British Parliament, be introduced? Victorians were so proud of their own institutions that they believed they should be exported.

Then there was the question of population. Canada and Australia had plenty of land, and Britain had plenty of money for investment. To encourage settlers, land in Australia was sold at very low prices to British emigrants. It was generally accepted that these colonies, settled by Europeans, would in time break away from the mother country as the United States had done. This time, it was hoped, the break might be made in a more gradual and more friendly manner.

The new constitutional ideas were first put into effect in Canada, after Lord Durham's investigation of Canadian affairs in 1838, and the Canada Act of 1840 was the first step on the road to self-government. Many problems remained, including the hostility between French and English Canadians that still survives, but eventually a federal constitution was adopted and confirmed by the British Parliament in the British North America Act of 1867. With that act, the Dominion of Canada came into existence as a self-governing state acknowledging the sovereignty of the British crown.

Constitutional development in Australia was slower, because the population was smaller and widely scattered. A measure of democracy was introduced in 1842, and the population expanded rapidly after the discovery of gold. However, it was not until 1900 that Australia adopted a federal constitution and thus became a single, self-governing state under the British crown.

New Zealand progressed more rapidly, and although the title of "Dominion" was not granted until 1907, the country was self-governing in all but name as early as 1875.

South Africa presented the British government with a unique colonial problem. The colony at the Cape of Good Hope was bought from The Netherlands in the early years of the nineteenth century, and the majority of the European population was of Dutch descent. These people, known as Boers (farmers), were tough, independent-minded stock raisers who, for various reasons, disliked British rule. Shortly before Victoria came to the throne, about ten thousand of them moved northeast in the "Great Trek" to found new settlements away from British rule. Unlike the Cape Colony, the areas in which they settled—Natal, the Orange Free State, and the Transvaal—were dominated by a vigorous and warlike tribal people, the Zulus. The result was a succession of wars between Europeans and Africans. The British were unable to control the situation, and though they took over Natal as a colony in 1843, the Orange Free State and the Transvaal achieved independence.

The whole area remained unstable, with the Boers, the British, and the Africans all more or less hostile to each other, but no further divisions were made until the great burst of imperialist expansion in the last quarter of the century.

In the Dominions—Canada, Australia, and New Zealand—and in the Cape Colony, European colonists had rapidly swamped the native population. The original inhabitants of all those countries were comparatively few in number (except in New Zealand) and their societies were primitive by European standards. They were unable to defend themselves (they did not always want to) against the superior arms and organization of the Europeans, who seldom considered their interests. Apart from the South African Boers, the settlers were of British descent and, on the whole, loyal to the country of their origin.

In India the situation was entirely different. That vast country was already thickly populated when the British arrived, and it possessed a cultural history older than that of Europe. No attempt was made at colonial settlement. The British came in search of trade, and until the middle of the nineteenth century it was a commercial corporation, the British East India Company, and not the British government, that administered most Indian affairs.

The large Indian population, which included many different peoples, was of course completely alien to the British. Christianity, parliamentary institutions, capitalism—these meant nothing to the Indians. Although the civilization of India was very old it was, to European eyes, a very impractical sort of civilization. Science, industry, and technology had no part in it; it was unscientific and nonmaterialistic. As the historian and politician Thomas Macaulay crudely said, Indian "history" abounded with kings 30 feet high and reigns 30,000 years long, while Indian "geography" had seas made of treacle or butter.

Many British officials in India were intelligent men who did not wish to damage Indian civilization. However, the confrontation of two such different cultures had certain profound and inevitable results.

It was obviously desirable to have a single language in India, but if one of the major Indian languages were adopted, only the knowledge and literature of that one language would become available. There were obvious reasons for choosing English. So the British became the teachers of the Indians. They taught them English in order to teach them the benefits of British customs, British products, and British techniques. And with the best intentions, the British found it impossible not to interfere with traditional Indian society. For example, they could not condone the Hindu practice of burning widows along with their husbands' bodies.

Once the British became teachers, they were bound to become rulers, and this development was assisted by the Indian caste system. As time went by, the number of British administrators and officials increased; they brought their wives out from England and formed little communities of their own. They became cut off from the Indian population and grew ever more convinced of their own superiority. In 1824 the governor of the state of Madras had looked forward to a time when "it will probably be best for both countries that the British control over India should be gradually withdrawn." Fifty years later, very few Englishmen ever considered such a possibility.

Nevertheless, until 1857 relations between the British and the Indian population remained quite amiable. Despite some minor wars, the British believed that their rule was not resented, for nationalism in the European sense did not exist in India. The event that drastically changed the political atmosphere was the Indian Mutiny, which broke out in May, 1857.

The immediate cause of the outbreak was the objection of Indian soldiers to the practice of lubricating cartridges with animal fat, which was offensive to both the Hindu and Muslim religions. But there were deeper causes than this. The British had ignored many Indian traditions, and Hindus felt that the existence of their religion was threatened by British social reforms.

The mutiny spread throughout the army (in which Indians outnumbered British soldiers by six to one) and it was not suppressed for over a year. Terrible atrocities were committed by both sides, and in Britain the public screamed for vengeance. The governor-general of India, Lord Canning, earned the honorable nickname of "Clemency," but his restraint and tolerance made him unpopular with the British, though Queen Victoria backed him to the hilt.

The mutiny hardened the division between British and Indians in India. Thereafter, Indian soldiers enlisted in the British army were not completely trusted, and the proportion of British soldiers was increased. Distrust extended to other classes, although civilians had not played any part in the mutiny. The British became more and more a ruling class, and the Indians became "second-class citizens."

One good result of the mutiny, warmly welcomed by Queen Victoria, was that the authority of the East India Company was ended, and all British India came under the crown. Benjamin Disraeli had always advocated this change. One can only act on Eastern peoples, Disraeli said, through their imagination. A trading company was a dull sort of authority; a great monarch would be much more effective. Further development of this idea had to wait until Disraeli became prime minister.

Queen Victoria once confessed to "a great longing sometime to go to India," but, though her sons traveled in all the British Dominions, the queen herself never went farther than the European continent. She admired the vigor of British colonials, and she thought it might be a good idea if junior members of the royal family settled in Canada or Australia. Indeed, it might be necessary, for she never forgot that European crowns had tumbled in the revolutions of 1848 and that the future of royalty could not be guaranteed. Republicanism was still a popular doctrine in many quarters. That was why Victoria said that royal children ought to receive an education that would fit them for a more democratic society.

Yet these sensible ideas were quickly forgotten whenever it was suggested that the Prince of Wales should travel abroad. Victoria never liked him to leave England, not even to cross the Irish Sea, and she still harbored doubts about his reliability: he might not behave with the dignity necessary in the heir to the throne. Besides, the queen felt that he rushed about far too much when he was in England. "The country and all of *us*," she told him sternly, "would like to see you a little more stationary."

Nevertheless, the prince did persuade his mother to let him make a tour of India in 1875, partly because the trip was organized so quickly that Victoria had no time to think of convincing reasons why he should not go. The tour was a great success, and the queen forgot all her misgivings when he returned with gifts and tributes from the Indian princes, and full of stories of her personal popularity. Best of all, he brought back for her a superbly bound edition of Victoria's *Leaves from the Journal* translated into Hindustani.

Queen Victoria's feelings about the British Empire, like her feelings about many other subjects, were an odd mixture that cannot be explained by any logical principle. One reason why she preferred Disraeli to Gladstone was that Disraeli promised an active part for Britain abroad, while Gladstone's foreign policy was, in the queen's eyes, negative if not feeble. She was too sensible to like war; she hated conquest—and bitterly criticized Prussia's aggressive expansion in Europe. On the other hand, she was aware that war has its glorious moments, and she approved of all the feelings (not bad in themselves) that make war and conquest more likely: pride, patriotism, the refusal to compromise or, in her words, "knuckle under." Like most of her subjects she believed that "British is best," and this feeling was becoming stronger in Britain in the 1870's, encouraged by Disraeli's forceful foreign policy. The word "jingoism," which means an aggressive sort of patriotism, came into use during this period.

THE BRITISH EMPIRE

What was the justification for the British Empire? Queen Victoria thought it was to help the peoples of the undeveloped lands, to bring them the benefits of Western (and particularly British) civilization, and to "protect" them. By "protection," the queen meant the building of hospitals and schools as well as the teaching of the Christian religion and Victorian morality. Her ideas were too simple, and today's African nationalists would scoff at them, quite rightly. But in her time the world was different; for one thing, there were no African nationalists.

When war broke out in the colonies, Victoria tended to sympathize with the rebels. How else could one expect these poor people to behave, when the white races set such a disgraceful example?

While Victoria had some odd ideas, racism was not one of them. She tried hard to end segregation in the British army, but public opinion (and the commander in chief) were against her. She was always delighted to receive kings and chieftains from the imperial territories, some of whom made an astonishing spectacle in the sedate surroundings of the English court. Once, for example, she received a sincere, though unusual, greeting from an African chief who expressed the hope that her blanket might never be infested with fleas. She accepted the greeting with a perfectly straight face.

Of all the many and varied peoples who acknowledged Queen Victoria as their sovereign, her favorites (after the Scots) were the Indians. She shared the fascination that many English people felt for the ancient culture of India, and she could not help being impressed by the fantastic richness of the lives of many Indian princes, evidence of which frequently arrived in the form of lavish gifts. Probably she was also influenced by the strikingly good looks of many Indians, for Victoria was always an admirer of handsome people.

CHAPTER XII

Empress of India

In 1874 Benjamin Disraeli traveled down to Osborne for his first royal audience as prime minister since his brief spell of office in 1868. The queen, smiling with delight, received him as if he were a knight on a white charger come to rescue her—and the country—from the clutches of the demon Gladstone. The Conservative leader, in appearance at least, hardly fitted such a romantic role, but despite gout and asthma he was still, in the queen's eyes, a conquering hero. She invited him to be seated in her presence, and though he refused on this first occasion, he afterward always sat during royal interviews—the only minister except Lord Melbourne to achieve this breach of the queen's stiff etiquette.

Gladstone thought, unjustly, that Disraeli helped

to prejudice the queen against him, and he privately accused his rival of encouraging her to take a larger part in political affairs than the constitution permitted. Gladstone would never have told the queen the intimate details of cabinet meetings as Disraeli did, and he would never have told her that she had the right to dismiss her ministers when they displeased her. But Gladstone could not understand the romantic game which Disraeli and the queen played. Whatever he said, Disraeli would not have allowed the government to be dismissed at the queen's whim, just as Victoria, when she threatened to abdicate the throne, did not expect to be taken seriously. Gladstone's accusations of constitutional misconduct were based on suspicion rather than serious evidence.

Disraeli had promised that a Conservative government would conduct the affairs of the British Empire with more boldness than the Liberals had shown. In 1875 an opportunity appeared for him to demonstrate exactly what he meant.

The opening of the Suez Canal in 1869 had been an important event for Britain because it halved the distance of the voyage from England to India. Ships that before had sailed the whole length of the African continent around the Cape could now cut through to the Indian Ocean via the Mediterranean and the Red Sea. The Suez Canal had been built by a Frenchman, and though more British ships used it than all other nations combined, it was owned half by French businessmen and half by the khedive of Egypt.

In 1875 the inefficient government of the khedive was nearing bankruptcy; it had exhausted its international credit and had no other sources of income. The shares it owned in the Suez Canal Company had never brought much profit, so the khedive decided to sell them to the French.

Some unofficial diplomatic breeze blew word of his intention to the British government, and Disraeli saw immediately what a splendid thing it would be for Great Britain to get the shares. But the obstacles were formidable. A huge sum of money was involved, and the khedive needed it within three weeks. Such a sum could only be obtained through a special grant of Parliament, but Parliament was not in session and could not be assembled in time. Disraeli thought of a startling alternative—to borrow the money from his good friend Lord Rothschild, head of the great merchant bank.

It was highly unorthodox to borrow money from a private source, but, as Disraeli said, he could certainly offer good security—the British government! Rothschild agreed, and the purchase was made. Disraeli rattled off an exultant message to the queen: "You have it, Madam." The grateful queen noted in her journal: "An immense thing ... entirely Mr. Disraeli's doing."

The acquisition of the Suez Canal shares safeguarded the route to India and, as a pleasant incidental benefit, brought in a fine profit as the shares rose in value. But for Disraeli and the queen, it was above all a grand gesture. Neither of them spared much thought for the economic aspect.

Disraeli liked to pretend that Victoria was an all-powerful monarch and himself as prime minister no more than her servant. This was part of his romantic attitude toward the throne which, as a rule, had very little effect on his actual conduct of government. There were times, however, when pressure by Victoria forced him into actions he would rather have avoided. The crisis over the Public Worship Bill was one such occasion.

The purpose of this bill, which was initiated in the House of Lords by the archbishop of Canterbury, was to end certain practices in the "High Church" sect of the Church of England, which seemed dangerously close to Roman Catholicism. Disraeli wanted nothing to do with the bill; his cabinet included at least one High Church member (Lord Salisbury), and he anticipated much ill feeling for little purpose.

The queen, whose religious sympathies tended toward the Low Church party, urged government support for the bill. Disraeli at first resisted, but the queen was inexorable. Reluctantly, but gracefully, he surrendered, and once he had thrown the weight of the government behind the bill, it was passed fairly easily.

Although harsh words were spoken, a cabinet split was avoided, and Disraeli breathed freely once again.

A more striking example of the queen's influence on the government was the Royal Titles Act of 1876. Ever since India had been brought under the crown in 1858, Victoria had felt that she ought to have a title to signify this new responsibility. "Empress of India" sounded splendid, and surely Mr. Disraeli, who had often spoken of the importance of royal prestige in India, would agree? Her brother rulers in Russia and Germany were called emperors; were they greater than she? Also, such a title would show the Russians that Britain meant to hold on to India and would not be intimidated by the expanding Russian power beyond the Himalayas.

The queen's enthusiasm was kindled afresh by the Prince of Wales' visit to India, and she urged the prime minister to bring a Royal Titles bill before Parliament. In principle, Disraeli was willing, but public opinion was unfavorable. The rulers of England had been kings or queens for a thousand years: Why should Victoria suddenly want such an un-English title as empress?

As a gesture of support, the queen agreed to open Parliament in person in 1876, but this did not make the prime minister's job any easier when he introduced the bill to make her an empress. Both in the Commons and in the Lords, the bill was fiercely criticized. Victoria took the attacks personally and was by turns irritated, upset, and enraged. She refused to yield to *"mere* clamour and intimidation," and after a long and hectic debate, the Royal Titles Act passed into law. One of its provisions stated that the imperial title should refer to India alone, but Victoria never paid much attention to that restriction. Writing to Disraeli, she signed herself with a bold flourish: "V.R.& I." *(Victoria Regina et Imperatrix*—Queen and Empress).

At Delhi, the queen's new title was proclaimed in a splendid ceremony attended by many of the Indian princes and rajahs. As the viceroy reported: "There can be no question of the complete success of this great Imperial ceremony"; and he added, "The weather has been most favourable." Victoria received his message with "the greatest satisfaction and pleasure" but offered no comment on the climate in London.

Her distress at the opposition to her imperial title might have been spared her if she had been forewarned of public opinion. Unfortunately, her courtiers and ministers from Lord Melbourne onward always tended to paint the political scene in a rosy light, and when events turned out less favorably, the queen was unprepared. As time went by and the queen became an ever more formidable figure, the people around her found frankness more and more difficult. Few were those who dared provoke a royal tantrum (she was capable of angrily sweeping the ornaments off a table when quite an old lady), and many of those who could have spoken out had passed from the scene. The younger generation were naturally intimidated more easily. Yet, as her secretary said, when the true situation was explained to her in a clear and reasonable way, she usually accepted it calmly. Those who told her only what they thought she wanted to hear merely stored up trouble for the future.

The poor health of the prime minister made him decide to accept a peerage in 1876, and bidding farewell to the House of Commons, Disraeli took his seat as Lord Beaconsfield in the House of Lords. After the ordeal of the Royal Titles Act, the queen thought he needed a rest, and the political atmosphere in the House of Lords was less strenuous than in the Commons. The world, however, and in particular the Turks, the Russians, and Mr. Gladstone, were not prepared to let him rest for long. The Turkish problem, which had been simmering since the Crimean War, erupted in a diplomatic crisis that suddenly threatened a full-scale European war.

The Christian subjects of the Turks in the Balkan countries, restless under alien rule, rebelled against their corrupt and oppressive masters in 1875–76. With the desperation of a declining power, the Turks retaliated savagely. Whole villages in Bulgaria were destroyed and their inhabitants—men, women, and children—were brutally murdered. News of these horrors shocked the British public, and Gladstone, emerging from retirement like an angry Moses descending from Mount Sinai, fanned anti-Turkish feeling with his famous pamphlet, *The Bulgarian Horrors and the Question of the East,* a propaganda masterpiece of righteous anger and fierce invective, which sold 200,000 copies in a month.

The British government was in an awkward position. They could not defend the ghastly actions of the Turks, but they feared that Russia would use the Bulgarian "horrors" as an excuse to destroy the Turkish Empire and make themselves masters of the Middle East. Russian troops were already on the move and, once again, India seemed to be in danger.

A conference was held at Constantinople, where the powers of Europe worked out an agreement—only for the Turks to reject its terms. Russia prepared for invasion. The queen, ferociously anti-Russian, urged strong measures on the British government, while Disraeli wished that Russians and Turks were all at the bottom of the Black Sea.

During the summer of 1877, the steady advance of the Russian army stilled anti-Turkish cries in England. The heroic defense by a small Turkish garrison of the town of Plevna swung popular feeling toward the Turks, and the government, blamed for its pro-Turkish policy the year before, was now attacked for feebleness toward Russia. The queen demanded action: "Pray do beware of *delay,* for the state of Turkey is most alarming . . . every *hour* is *precious.*"

Disraeli himself was held back by divisions among his colleagues in the cabinet, but when Lord Salisbury became foreign secretary he gained powerful support for a militant policy. The British fleet sailed for Constantinople, and regiments of the Indian army were moved into the Mediterranean area.

Nobody wanted another Crimean War—certainly not the British government, who this time could not rely on the alliance of France. After several weeks of acute tension, an armistice was signed by the Russians and the Turks, and the whole problem was referred to an international congress that met in Berlin in the summer of 1878.

Disraeli in person led the British delegation. In the course of two months of tough negotiations he secured what was, for Britain, a very satisfactory settlement. Russia was kept out of the Middle East; Bulgaria gained its independence, and the Turkish state, though reduced, was not destroyed. When he returned from the congress, Disraeli told the crowd waiting to greet him that he had brought back "peace with honor." It was a fair summing-up of the event that marked the climax of his long career and raised British prestige in Europe to a level it had not reached even in the days of Lord Palmerston.

The queen greeted her returning hero at Osborne, offering him the highest honors she could give. Disraeli refused them all but the exclusive and ancient Order of the Garter. Sitting in the garden at Osborne, he kept the queen amused for hours with anecdotes, some of them scandalous, about the Berlin congress.

The Congress of Berlin sorted out the problems of Europe, and its settlement was not seriously disturbed until long after Victoria's death. But Europe was a relatively small part of the huge area of the world that directly concerned the British government. As the queen wrote to Disraeli: ". . . we must, with our Indian Empire and large Colonies, be *prepared* for *attacks* and *wars, somewhere or other,* CONTINU-ALLY."

In South Africa, the continued hostility between the Boers and the Zulus was creating conditions of near anarchy. The government decided that the only solution was for Britain to step in and form a federation of the various South African territories like the successful federation of Canada. The Transvaal was formally annexed as a first step. A settlement with the Zulus was worked out, but the British governor of the Cape unwisely insisted that the Zulu army should be disbanded. To the Zulus, this meant the destruction of their whole way of life. They rose against the British, who now found both the Boers and the Africans against them. The Zulu war began with an unexpected victory for the Zulus at Isandwhalla, but spears could not long prevail against guns, and in July, 1879, the Zulu army was shattered.

The Zulu war was expensive and, many people thought, unjust. Though the British governor had acted against advice from London, the Disraeli government was naturally blamed.

A simultaneous campaign in Afghanistan also seemed morally wrong. That mountainous kingdom divided British India from Russia, and the British were highly sensitive to Russian influence at Kabul, the Afghan capital. In 1878 a Russian mission was received by the Afghan government, and the viceroy of India, Lord Lytton, immediately demanded equal representation for the British. He won his point but at the cost of antagonizing the Afghans who, in September, 1879, rose and massacred the entire British mission at Kabul. Coming only six months after the news of the Zulu victory at Isandwhalla, the Kabul disaster deeply shocked the British public. The queen expressed her horror and distress: "How could it happen?"

Prestige demanded the immediate restoration of British influence, so British units of the Indian army invaded Afghanistan. As in South Africa, the British government had not been in control of events. Policy was decided by the official on the spot, in this case the viceroy of India. However, any government must take responsibility for acts committed in its name.

The wars in South Africa and in Afghanistan were, on the face of it, typically "imperialist" actions, and they ended in more power and more territory for Britain. But they did not begin as wars of conquest; on the contrary, the chief motive behind them was defensive. Moreover, the government in London did not start them, and Disraeli was annoyed with both the South African governor and the Indian viceroy whose impetuous actions had helped to provoke these conflicts. Finally, both wars were unpopular in England, where many people sympathized with the Zulus and the Afghans.

Gladstone made the most of the dissatisfaction. He was the first British politician to approach the voters directly in the time-honored American manner, by stumping the country, making speeches at each stopping place. His theme was the foreign policy of the Conservative government, which he fiercely condemned as aggressive, immoral, useless, and expensive. He was an orator of charismatic power, and his speeches had a tremendous effect.

The queen was disgusted by his behavior. Not only was she a supporter of Disraeli's foreign policy, but she resented Gladstone's popularity with the masses. "The People's William" he was called. Victoria had always liked to think of herself as "the People's Victoria." And here was Gladstone standing up for African natives and Afghan tribesmen; that, too, had always been her prerogative—or so she thought.

Just how effective Gladstone was in rousing the public against the Disraeli government was made plain by the result of the parliamentary election of 1880. The Liberals won by a landslide.

As Gladstone was not the official leader of the

Liberal party (he had "retired" in 1874), the queen hoped for a moment that he would not have to be prime minister. She tried every possible alternative, but no Liberal leader would agree to form a government without Gladstone, and Gladstone would not accept any position except prime minister. Thus Victoria bowed to the inevitable, and summoned the man she called a "half-mad fire-brand" to Windsor.

Meanwhile, the wizened figure of Disraeli, wrapped up in rugs, was driven from the prime minister's residence for the last time. A little over a year later he was dead. The queen erected a memorial to him in the church where he was buried, which carried a quotation from the Bible: "Kings love him that speaketh right." Mr. Gladstone, if he saw it, might have read there an unspoken rebuke to himself.

CHAPTER XIII

Tragedy in Khartoum

By the late 1870's Victoria was a calmer and stronger person than she had ever been. Although the royal physicians still sometimes feared a nervous breakdown, the emotional strains of the 1860's had almost vanished. Victoria's journal was no longer filled with complaints about her "miserable existence." She was again recording her determined efforts to correct what she regarded as faults in her own character.

While Victoria was never a "shrinking violet," she still suffered at times from a lack of confidence in herself. Her exalted position naturally demanded a greater degree of self-confidence than is required from humbler folk. At the beginning of her reign, Lord Melbourne had helped her overcome her anxiety;

later, Albert had been there to support and guide her. The shattering experience of his death had made her feel that she could not carry on, and her refusal to play any part in public life was partly a result of her feeling of inadequacy. Time brought some improvement; then Disraeli became prime minister, and she was surrounded by an atmosphere of respectful adoration. Six years of this treatment effected a more or less permanent cure.

In 1879, the year that saw the birth of the queen's first great-grandchild, Victoria turned sixty. She had been queen for over forty years; very few men in England had been in public life so long a time. Politicians who lectured her seriously on some issue of the moment felt rather crushed when the queen responded by telling them what Lord Melbourne or the Duke of Wellington had said on the subject. Her prestige was enormous, and her name was venerated by people who had never come within a thousand miles of England and had only the vaguest idea of what "England" or "the queen" meant. Planters in Africa, soldiers in the Far East, officials in Canada and Australasia—all drank to the health of Her Majesty.

Victoria was aware of this veneration, but she never gave it much thought; she simply took it for granted! Yet, at the same time, she worried about the health of her servants and went round visiting the Balmoral cottagers in an old bonnet that cost no more than a dollar.

The vein of toughness, which had been evident in the young princess, had grown more marked in the elderly queen. She herself recognized that in some ways she was better fitted to deal with life's blows than Albert had been. She no longer judged every act by what Albert would have wished. Near Balmoral Castle she had a house built that was smaller and "cozier." This became her favorite residence, although it had never been blessed with the presence of the prince consort. And what would Albert have thought if he could have seen the queen, bothered by flies on a picnic, puffing away at a cigarette?

Times changed, as the queen herself often noted—usually with regret. Professor Alexander Graham Bell arrived one day in 1878 to demonstrate his new invention, the telephone. Victoria remarked that it made a horrid noise and was "rather faint." Nor did she care for the inventor, who, she considered, was much too pleased with himself.

As the queen's prestige and confidence expanded, those who were close to her, including her own children, did not find her an easier person to deal with. Indeed, nearly everyone was a little afraid of her formidable personality. Her opinions—whether about child-rearing or constitutional reform—were not easily shaken.

Her judgments of people were increasingly frank. For example, the wife of President Ulysses S. Grant was "civil and complimentary" but in a "funny American way," while the President's son was "a very ill-mannered young Yankee." Americans, the queen thought, though admirable people in their way, were not always respectable and even a little crude. Of course, they did not have the advantage of a constitutional monarch to set them a good example.

At times Victoria behaved in a manner that was thoughtless or downright selfish. Her youngest daughter, Princess Beatrice, was her chief support, and she did not welcome the prospect of losing this beloved child to some eligible prince. In the queen's lonely situation such a feeling was natural, but Victoria took excessive precautions to prevent the girl from meeting a likely young man. No one was allowed to mention the word "wedding," and poor Beatrice could not talk about ordinary family affairs, with their suggestion of children and therefore husbands, without incurring a frown from her mother.

Nevertheless, the queen's attempts to keep the princess a spinster failed in the end, and Beatrice married a German prince—on the important condition that the young couple would continue to live with the queen. As things turned out, Beatrice's charming husband became Victoria's favorite son-in-law, and nobody mourned his tragically early death more than she.

One of the saddest experiences of growing old is to see one's friends and relatives gradually dying off. At times, Victoria's life seemed to be one long succession of sad deaths. She had already lost one child, Princess Alice, in 1878, and in 1884 Prince Leopold, the most delicate of her children, died only a few months after his marriage. Disraeli went in 1881 and two years later he was followed by another old friend who, in some ways, was even closer to the queen—John Brown. To the consternation of the court, Victoria wanted to publish a memoir about her beloved Scots steward; but the dean of Windsor persuaded her not to, and was surprised not to lose his job as a result. Instead, the queen bestowed on her fascinated subjects another volume of *Leaves* from her journal of life in the Highlands.

In the years between 1880 and 1885, Victoria needed all her toughness and courage, for besides the succession of deaths in her private circle, public affairs required her close attention: Mr. Gladstone was once more prime minister and his policies incurred her disapproval.

Gladstone's second ministry was less successful than his first, partly because he lacked a comprehensive program, and partly because of circumstances beyond the government's control. Ireland's state was again desperate after agricultural depression in the late 1870's. Over ten thousand tenants were thrown off their land for failure to pay rents in 1880 alone. Violence reached a new pitch: houses and haystacks were burned, men beaten and stabbed, and, the crowning blow, the chief secretary for Ireland, Lord Frederick Cavendish, was assassinated in Dublin. Reluctantly Gladstone agreed to a coercion act, meeting force with force. He followed it with a new land act, but this reform was not sufficient to satisfy the Irish.

Eventually, the Irish "Home Rulers" (those who wanted an independent Ireland) withdrew their support from the Liberals and formed an alliance with Lord Randolph Churchill, leader of an aggressive "ginger group" in the Conservative party. Their action destroyed the Liberal majority in the House of Commons and led to the defeat of Gladstone's government in 1885.

At times, the Grand Old Man, as Gladstone was sometimes called, feared that the days of parliamentary democracy in Britain were numbered. The Irish and Lord Randolph Churchill were not the only disruptive elements. Gladstone's supporters were divided between old-fashioned Whigs—the political descendants of Lord Melbourne and his ilk—and Radicals like Sir Charles Dilke (who had once called for the abolition of the monarchy) and Joseph Chamberlain, the powerful spokesman for the prosperous industrialist class. Radical pressure persuaded Gladstone that fundamental political reform was overdue.

Political reform was one of the great themes of nineteenth-century England. When Victoria was born, only a tiny minority of Englishmen had the right to vote. The franchise was widened by the Great Reform Act of 1832 and subsequent minor changes. Another large stride was taken with Disraeli's Reform Act of 1867, which extended the vote to the more prosperous members of the working class. The effect of Gladstone's act of 1884 was, roughly, to give the vote to all adult male citizens (women remained voteless).

None of these steps toward democracy was taken without fierce opposition, and Gladstone's act was no exception. It produced a serious constitutional crisis in which the queen, for almost the last time, invaded the political battlefield with flags flying and royal guns blazing.

The reform bill passed the House of Commons but was rejected by the predominantly Conservative House of Lords on a rather technical point. At this, the Radicals among Gladstone's supporters launched a massive attack on the institution of the House of Lords. "Peers versus people" was their battle cry. This was the very danger that normally prevented the Lords from risking a direct clash with the Commons.

Victoria, who cared less about the reform bill than about the House of Lords, now entered the lists. First she urged Gladstone to restrain his fiercer followers. Next she turned her guns on Lord Salisbury, the Conservative leader in the House of Lords. He must not, she said, resist the principle of reform, however much he disliked the terms of Gladstone's bill. Lord Salisbury offered polite but firm resistance. Gladstone, in a rare moment of tact, expressed an unexpected desire to leave the whole affair in the queen's "skilled and experienced hands."

Victoria succeeded in enlisting the service of two moderates in the House of Lords to work on Lord Salisbury, while she tried to undermine support for Joseph Chamberlain and the Radicals in the Commons. The prime minister did not help matters at this stage by making some inflammatory speeches in Scotland, and Victoria aimed a broadside in his direction: "The Queen is *utterly* disgusted with his *stump* oratory." (The message reached Gladstone in the more tactful wording of the queen's private secretary.)

Counsels of peace at last prevailed. Gladstone suggested a compromise that met some of the Lords' objections to his bill, and Lord Salisbury, under royal pressure, agreed to it. The foreign secretary in a letter to the queen, remarked that "your Majesty must feel rather proud of the powerful influence which your Majesty has brought to bear upon the probable settlement of this burning question," and Victoria justly noted in her journal, "I certainly am."

When Gladstone took over as prime minister in 1880, the queen impressed upon him that no changes should be made in foreign policy. This was a very

TRAGEDY IN KHARTOUM

unreasonable demand, because it was largely Disraeli's foreign policy that had caused the Conservatives' election defeat. Moreover, Gladstone hated Disraeli's foreign policy and had often said so.

However, whether he liked it or not, Gladstone could not easily cast aside the mantle of imperialism passed on to him by his predecessor. The South African problem remained to be solved, and the Afghan war was still in progress.

The Boers expected the Liberal government to carry out its preelection promises by restoring independence to the Transvaal. But there was a delay, and the Boers, losing patience, resorted to arms. They defeated a British detachment in a minor battle, and the British public, its dignity affronted, demanded revenge. Wisely, Gladstone held out for peace and granted independence to the Transvaal in 1881.

Victoria bitterly resented this "surrender," not only because she did not like, as she once said, "giving things up," but also because of her concern for the African population. With some justice, she complained that they were being abandoned to the Boers, whom she called "a most merciless and cruel neighbour, and in fact oppressor."

The Afghan problem solved itself more easily, thanks to a successful British campaign by General Roberts. The Afghan government agreed to permit British control of its foreign affairs in return for a

177

subsidy, and the British forces, whose presence in Afghanistan Gladstone had vigorously denounced, were then withdrawn.

The Liberal government was also bound by Disraeli's arrangements at the Congress of Berlin (1878), one result of which was that Britain had been given Cyprus. At the time, Gladstone described this acquisition as "insane . . . an act of duplicity not surpassed and rarely equalled in the history of nations." Now that he was in power, he did not know what to do with Cyprus. He wanted to give it to Greece, but his foreign secretary persuaded him that Parliament would never agree. So Cyprus remained British.

Gladstone's policy of what the queen regarded as "retreat" did not please her. Mr. Gladstone, she feared, altogether lacked Mr. Disraeli's "very lofty views" of Britain's place in the world, and his whole cabinet seemed incompetent and unruly.

The prime minister admitted that his relations with the queen had become almost intolerable. He found himself fighting a continual battle "on the side of liberty as opposed to Jingoism." It seemed hardly possible that things could get worse, but Gladstone's handling of troubles in Egypt and the Sudan was to bring crown and prime minister perilously close to a public quarrel.

The sale of the Suez Canal shares in 1875 had not solved the financial difficulties of the Egyptian government, which had gone bankrupt a year later.

Neither the French nor the British, both of whom had important financial interests in Egypt (including the canal), could afford to let that country fall into chaos. The Disraeli government had therefore arranged a system of joint Anglo-French control of Egypt's financial affairs.

This clumsy arrangement did not last long. In 1881 Egyptian nationalists rebelled against the government of the khedive, whom they accused of being the puppet of the Europeans. Once more, Egypt slumped toward anarchy.

Some action by the controlling powers was clearly necessary, but the French government was involved in a domestic crisis and would not commit itself to any decisive action. To save Egypt from complete economic collapse, it was necessary to restore peace quickly, and Gladstone, seeing no other alternative, gave the very un-Gladstonian order for the British fleet to bombard Alexandria, which was held by the rebels. Subsequently, a British force defeated the rebels on land and occupied Cairo.

Thus the system of indirect control over Egypt, exercised in cooperation with France, ended in direct control exercised by Britain alone. Gladstone had apparently revived Disraeli's policy of imperial expansion, and in a particularly aggressive form. He hoped to withdraw from Egypt as soon as order was fully restored, but that was easier said than done.

Egypt itself was not a very large country, for there

were no large settlements except on the coast and along the Nile River. But behind Egypt lay the vast expanse of the Sudan, unmapped, seldom visited, and generally ignored.

The Egyptian administration of the Sudan had been corrupt and inefficient. Discontent seethed among the tribes. The country was ripe for revolt, and in 1881 it found the necessary leader in the Mahdi (an Arabic title meaning, roughly, "the Prophet"). This mysterious figure emerged from the desert and proved to be a charismatic religious leader who swiftly gathered supporters from a wide area. Within two years the Mahdi was the virtual ruler of the Sudan. When the Egyptian government sent a force of ten thousand men to crush him, under the command of a British officer, Colonel Hicks, the Mahdi's forces annihilated Hicks and his entire army in one bloody battle.

The last thing Gladstone wanted was to extend British involvement into the Sudan; but the queen insisted that Hicks should be avenged and, as usual, she voiced the feelings of a majority of her subjects. Gladstone conceded that at least Britain might help to evacuate the remaining Egyptian garrisons in the Sudan which had not yet fallen to the Mahdi's murderous hordes. The man appointed to undertake this delicate operation was General Charles George ("Chinese") Gordon, a highly unorthodox commander who had made a great name for himself in China and, later, during a tour of duty in the Sudan.

The story of Gordon and the Sudan is riddled with mistakes, omissions, doubts, and carelessness, the end of which was the tragedy of Khartoum in 1885.

Gladstone's opponents sometimes accused him of acting as if he were God. But General Gordon, in a strange way, really did believe in his own divine mission in life. He despised the life of "society," loathed "fine ladies," and cared for no woman except his sister and few men except himself. His military achievements were certainly brilliant: He seemed to have an almost miraculous command over the most undisciplined men, and he had been known to quell a violent riot with no weapons except his officer's cane and the compelling gaze of his peculiarly blue eyes. Like another, later British military hero of unorthodox methods, Lawrence of Arabia, Gordon's success depended finally on the extraordinary power of his will.

As a leader of irregular troops in an aggressive war Gordon was unequaled. But as the man to carry out a withdrawal that was likely to require diplomacy and self-effacement he was a disaster. He once wrote in his diary, "I know if *I* was chief, I would never employ *myself,* for I am incorrigible."

Gladstone, who had never met Gordon, agreed that he should be sent out to report on the situation of the Egyptian garrisons—no more than that. Gordon thought, probably with sincerity, that his orders went much further. And in any case, as he admitted, he had never been noted for sticking to orders.

Queen Victoria welcomed Gordon's appointment, and inquired ironically why it had not been made at an earlier stage in the crisis. But she was soon worrying about his safety. As early as February, 1884, she remarked to the prime minister, "If anything befalls *him* [Gordon], the result will be awful."

In the same month, Gordon reached Khartoum, the capital of the Sudan, and had himself declared governor-general. The British government, their decisions hampered by slow communications, wondered why he should feel this title was necessary just to evacuate the garrisons. Next came a message saying that in Gordon's opinion it was important to restore some sort of government in the Sudan before evacuation. In other words, Gordon wanted to tackle the Mahdi head on. Unfortunately he had no army, but that deficiency would no doubt be remedied by the British government.

In March, the forces of the Mahdi closed in on Khartoum. Communications became unreliable, but it was clear that Gordon was in danger of being cut off. The queen asked whether a relieving force, perhaps sent from India, should not be prepared. Gladstone still hoped that Gordon would withdraw, according to his orders, but withdrawal was rapidly becoming impossible. As the weeks passed, the queen became more and more alarmed, but Gladstone refused to be drawn any further into the quagmire of the Sudan.

Public opinion echoed the queen's, and the government was severely criticized in Parliament. One member remarked that the whole country believed that Gordon was in danger except the prime minister. This peculiar situation, he went on, must be ascribed to Mr. Gladstone's powers of persuasion: "He can persuade most people of most things, and above all he can persuade himself of almost anything."

The drama approached its climax. Khartoum was surrounded, and communications ceased altogether. In August, after the whole cabinet had urged him to act, Gladstone at last agreed to send an army to save Khartoum. The preparations were carried out with dreadful slowness, and the 1,600-mile advance up the Nile was hampered by unexpectedly low water. The relieving force arrived on January 28, 1885, to find Khartoum in the possession of the Mahdi. General Gordon, together with thousands of the inhabitants, had been slaughtered just forty-eight hours before.

The queen, who had urged the government to send help almost a year before, was furiously angry and so upset that the cold she was suffering from turned into a fever. To the prime minister she sent a telegram: "These news from Khartoum are frightful, and to think that all might have been prevented and many precious lives saved by earlier action is too fearful."

The point about this telegram was that it was *not* sent in code, which was the usual practice, and the queen's rebuke to Gladstone could be read by any telegraph clerk through whose hands it passed. Whatever Gladstone's faults—and he cannot escape blame for Gordon's fate—the queen's action was insulting. Icily angry, the prime minister considered sending in his immediate resignation.

Gladstone's popularity slumped. The initials "G.O.M." (Grand Old Man) were reversed to read "M.O.G." (Murderer of Gordon). The prime minister was subjected to a campaign of abuse and contempt, and a few months later, when the Irish nationalists swung their support to the Conservatives, the Liberal government was defeated.

CHAPTER XIV

Golden Jubilee

After the Liberal defeat, the queen wrote to Mrs. Gladstone: "You must both rejoice at Mr. Gladstone's rest—which he so *often* spoke of as his *great* wish and which is essential at his time of life." Mrs. Gladstone cannot have failed to recognize Her Majesty's unspoken desire that Mr. Gladstone's "rest" should be permanent.

But at the general election of 1885 the Liberals won more seats than the Conservatives. The queen hoped that she might persuade right-wing Liberals to join the Conservatives in a coalition government that would keep Gladstone out of office, but the Grand Old Man would not be excluded. The queen had no alternative but to invite Gladstone to form his third ministry in February, 1886.

This time, Gladstone did not lack a program, for he had taken the most momentous political decision of his life. He had decided to support Home Rule for Ireland.

Irish independence was the aim of sixty-odd Irish members of the House of Commons, but they had, so far, made few allies among the English. Gladstone himself, though he had been deeply concerned with Ireland's troubles and had risked his political future more than once for the sake of improving Irish conditions, had never before admitted that independence was a possible solution. His conversion to Irish Home Rule astounded the country, horrified the queen, and set off the most violent political struggle of the age.

A leader of Gladstone's type arouses both violent hostility and passionate commitment. Benjamin Disraeli, a man whose attitude to individuals was usually tolerant, had loathed and despised Gladstone. The queen's feelings, of course, were no friendlier. On the other hand, Gladstone commanded intense loyalty from his friends.

Yet even his great gifts of leadership could not persuade the British Parliament to approve Home Rule. In a highly emotional debate, Gladstone made one of the finest speeches of his career: "Ireland stands at your bar, expectant, hopeful, almost suppliant . . . She asks a blessed oblivion of the past. . . . Think, I beseech you, think well, think wisely, think, not for the moment, but for the years that are to come, before you reject this Bill." At one hour after midnight, having spoken for three and a half hours, the seventy-six-year-old prime minister sat down. The vote was taken almost immediately: in favor, 313; against, 343.

Gladstone, from the best motives, had committed the same error of practical politics as Sir Robert Peel in 1846. He had adopted a policy which, though history later proved it right, his own party would not accept. The important difference was that Peel had succeeded in repealing the Corn Laws, but Gladstone failed to carry Home Rule. Shaken but unbeaten, Gladstone exercised the right of the government in power to hold a general election (though only six months had passed since the last one). A fierce campaign followed, and bitter words were spoken on both sides. Lord Randolph Churchill in particular attacked Gladstone viciously, but there was a suggestion of truth in his gibe about "an old man in a hurry." Gladstone did not help matters by distributing some violently worded telegrams to his supporters, and in the final result, the pro-Gladstone Liberals were heavily defeated. The Grand Old Man packed his bags and left for a quiet vacation among the monasteries of Bavaria. He had earned a holiday, but he spent most of his time earnestly discussing Home Rule with the monks.

With a sigh of relief, the queen welcomed back a Conservative government under Lord Salisbury. This cool and intelligent statesman—a descendant of Queen

Elizabeth's great minister, Robert Cecil—had none of the romance of Disraeli, but his policy, the queen thought approvingly, was thoroughly Disraelian. He promised an expanding empire, not a contracting one.

However, Lord Salisbury and Queen Victoria had not been strangers during Gladstone's short ministry of 1886, when the queen's loathing for Home Rule had led her into highly irregular conduct. She had corresponded occasionally with Lord Melbourne and Disraeli when they were out of office, but she had not discussed serious matters with either of them. Her correspondence with Lord Salisbury during the first half of 1886 was entirely different. She asked him bluntly what she should do to frustrate Home Rule, and she sent him Gladstone's private letters to herself.

The duty of the sovereign is to support the government of the day; Victoria's correspondence—not to say plotting—with the leader of the opposition, was thoroughly unconstitutional. Lord Salisbury himself, a politician of long experience, was of course no less to blame. This was the queen's worst lapse from constitutional correctness. Her record as a whole, in view of her sincere opinion that Gladstone's government was a national disaster, was fair.

Victoria would not have admitted that her correspondence with Lord Salisbury in 1886 was unconstitutional. She would have claimed the right to take advice from anyone she liked—including the leader of the opposition! Victoria seems to have thought that the rights of the sovereign depended on some form of divine right; she would have denied the doctrine that they depend on the agreement of the people. The learned commentaries of constitutional historians and lawyers were beyond her grasp, but her native common sense, which told her not to push her "rights" too far, served her as well as the most profound theories of the constitution.

"Fifty years today since I came to the Throne!" Victoria noted in her journal. It was June 20, 1887. "God has mercifully sustained me through many great trials and sorrows."

Throughout the empire, Queen Victoria's Golden Jubilee was celebrated with feasts and fireworks, ceremonies and speeches. Presents and tributes poured in from every corner of the globe. At Windsor Castle the queen awoke to a glorious sunny day—typical "queen's weather," people said, for it was odd how often the weather turned out fine for Victoria. After a leisurely private breakfast outside under the trees, the queen drove to the station where a train waited to take her to London. From Paddington Station she drove in an open carriage to Buckingham Palace. People thronged the streets and young men climbed lampposts for a better view, while flags fluttered from every upper window. The cheers were deafening.

At the palace, the royalty of Europe and Asia

waited to greet her. Kings and queens, princes and princesses, stood in bemedaled ranks, a colorful mass of plumes and sashes, purple and scarlet, blue and gold, all come to pay tribute to the matriarch of Europe. As the queen-empress was announced, the murmuring of regal gossip died away. Into the room came a short dumpy figure, walking with rheumatic stiffness and wearing a bonnet of English lace. She favored them with a slight smile, and they bowed deeply.

The queen feared that two days of constant celebrations would leave her dead with fatigue, but it was worth it to see how much she was loved. There was a thanksgiving service at Westminster Abbey, at which the choir sang the *Te Deum* composed by Prince Albert, and a dinner at the palace with over fifty royal personages present (the queen described it as "a large family dinner").

On the evening of June 21, the queen drove down to Windsor, where boys from Eton, England's most exclusive private school, appeared in an unscheduled torchlit procession. Dinner was interrupted, and the queen hurried out to the quadrangle to see them. "Thank you very much," she called out in her clear, bell-like voice.

The celebrations were not confined to London and Windsor. In every English village, jubilee bonfires were lit, and in every outpost of the empire, the royal toast was drunk. The British national anthem, "God

GOLDEN JUBILEE

Save the Queen," echoed across African plains and Indian passes. New York newspapers, which had dismissed Victoria's accession in a brief paragraph, splashed the Golden Jubilee across their front pages, and American clergymen in their Sunday sermons praised the English queen for the Christian simplicity of her family life.

In Calcutta, Indians watched a spectacular fireworks display. "The principal feature," the viceroy of India reported, "was the outline of your Majesty's head, traced in lines of fire, which unexpectedly burst on the vision of the astonished crowd. The likeness was admirable . . ." In Bombay and Madras the queen's picture was carried in procession through cheering crowds. Indian rajahs marked the anniversary with gifts of cash to the Imperial Institute, and the Thakur of Morvi rode a magnificent Indian steed up to the doors of Windsor Castle, where he presented it to the queen.

London schoolchildren were entertained by a carnival in Hyde Park. A balloon was sent up with "Victoria" painted on it. One young girl was heard explaining: "There's Queen Victoria going up to heaven." It was the sort of comical remark that children sometimes make, but it was also a sign of the almost legendary aura that was beginning to surround the venerable queen. That little girl's grandmother was probably barely old enough to have seen the coronation. There were comparatively few people in

191

England who could remember a time when Victoria had not been queen.

Queen Victoria had not looked forward to the jubilee celebrations with much enthusiasm, disliking the idea of what she called hustle and bustle. But the outpouring of affection and praise, much greater than she had expected, acted on her like a tonic, and her last lingering dread of public appearances disappeared. Despite painful rheumatism and failing eyesight, the queen in her seventies was in many ways more active than she had been in her forties.

Life at court, generally dull and stiff, became much livelier. Actors and musicians appeared at Windsor, and amateur theatricals, seldom performed since Albert's death, once more kept the ladies of the court amused—though the queen sharply crushed one tactless suggestion that they should stage the execution of Mary Queen of Scots.

A sign of a slight relaxation of the court's rigid moral standards was the decision to end the ban against divorced women—provided they were the innocent parties. Lord Salisbury advised against extending this privilege to foreign divorcées, "on account of the risk of admitting American women of light character."

During jubilee year, the queen acquired several Indian servants. They were handsome fellows, Victoria thought, with their dark glowing skins and colorful turbans. The opinion of the courtiers was that Indians made a pleasant change after all those kilted Scots, but they soon discovered that another "John Brown" was in their midst.

One of the Indians, a man called Abdul Karim, rapidly gained a special place in the queen's favor, and was given the title of "the Queen's Munshi" (clerk). He taught her Hindustani, prepared curried dishes for her, and explained the religion of Islam. Soon he was reading state papers and giving his advice on the administration of the India Office. Ministers and courtiers grumbled among themselves, the queen's private secretary sighed despairingly, and her children and grandchildren threw up their hands in dismay; all united in trying to keep the Munshi in his place. The queen refused to listen to them and ascribed all their arguments to "race prejudice."

Whatever the queen believed, the Munshi was not a very suitable person to take into her confidence. He was chiefly interested in improving his own position in the world, and with the queen behind him he suceeded despite the opposition of practically everyone else. John Brown at least was honest and devoted to Victoria. The Munshi was far from truthful and was devoted first and foremost to himself. However, his influence was not as dangerous as some people feared. He was not particularly intelligent and did not try to interfere in politics. His ambitions were harmless; he had no desire to become a power behind the imperial throne, only to acquire a modest estate in India.

The queen was delighted to learn about India from an Indian, but the Munshi was not the best teacher imaginable. One result of his influence was to prejudice the queen against Hindus (the Munshi was a Muslim). As this was a period of violent hostility between Muslims and Hindus, such a prejudice was especially unfortunate.

The Munshi was the center of various court rows until the late 1890's, but by that time nobody thought of him as more than a nuisance. The queen, too, realized that the Munshi's critics were not motivated only by jealousy and race prejudice. Gradually, he ceased to be so prominent a member of her intimate circle.

Like John Brown's, the Munshi's presence was most awkward when the queen traveled abroad. Foreign courts were not always willing to treat him with the respect that he and the queen thought was his due. Fortunately, when the queen visited Germany in 1888, the Munshi was not among the party.

The main reason for her visit was to see her eldest daughter, whose husband had just become emperor of Germany. Tragically, the emperor was already dying of cancer of the throat, and Victoria and her daughter were to be twin empresses for only a few months. There was also a family matter to settle—the proposed marriage of one of Victoria's numerous grandchildren. But the visit is most interesting because it saw the only meeting between two of the strongest personalities of the age: Queen Victoria and Prince Bismarck, the German chancellor.

Victoria had always distrusted and disliked Bismarck, and Bismarck, muttering angrily about "petticoat governments," had often complained of her hostile influence on his plans. But the momentous interview turned out surprisingly well. Bismarck emerged afterward, wiping the sweat from his brow and exlaiming, "That was a woman! One could do business with her!" And Victoria was pleasantly surprised that the Prussian ogre seemed "so amiable and gentle."

While she was in Berlin, she had an opportunity to say a few words of warning to her grandson Willy, soon to be the emperor William II. That unstable man treated her with a peculiar mixture of respectful affection and joking condescension. He once said that he wished he could open his veins to drain out all his English blood, and he was stupidly rude to his uncle, the Prince of Wales, whose amiable smoothness perhaps made him feel inferior. People said that only one person could keep William in order—his grandmother. Certainly he was a little awed by that elderly lady.

By now, Victoria's family was spread all over Europe and even to North America, where a daughter was married to the governor-general of Canada. Family affairs, it sometimes seemed, took up as much of her time as the British Empire. She was very much the senior member of European royalty and she presided over the affairs of her children and grandchildren with a mixture of motherly affection and strictness. As she grew older and calmer, she became more tolerant, though no less frank. If there was a row over a princess who wanted to marry a commoner, or a breakdown in a royal marriage, Victoria was usually on the side of common sense and humanity. She had little patience for the exaggerated sense of honor of the German branch of the family, and when Prince Willy expressed his scorn for the lowborn husband of Princess Beatrice, she exploded with wrath: "If the Queen of England thinks a person good enough for her daughter, what have other people got to say?" Indeed, such a question defied an answer.

Nor did age prevent Victoria from involving herself in the most ordinary domestic events. Princess Victoria of Battenberg, a granddaughter, arrived at Windsor Castle to have her baby in the middle of the Sudan crisis. The queen arranged everything, and on the day the baby was born, she sat by her granddaughter's bedside for ten hours. The baby, incidentally, was to grow up to be the grandmother of Prince Philip, the Duke of Edinburgh, consort of Queen Elizabeth II.

CHAPTER XV

Imperialism

Victoria refused to admit the weakness that comes with advancing age. She was surprised and annoyed to discover that she had dropped off to sleep while sitting in her chair after tea, and she grumbled that she could not get eyeglasses that suited her, although no spectacles could compensate for the cataract that was gradually blinding her. Her secretary, she complained, should not write so small, and why must he use such pale ink? As a result, the man tactfully got himself a pen with an extra-wide nib, and instead of blotting the ink, which made it fainter, he dried it in a little copper oven.

By now, Victoria was permanently lame and had to walk with a stick. Often she had to be carried upstairs, and she suffered spasms of backache which were fatiguing as well as painful. All this was "very tiresome," but her spirits remained buoyant. "May God enable me to become worthier . . ." she wrote in her journal on New Year's Day, 1891, "and may He preserve me yet for some years!" This was a very different woman from the pathetic creature of thirty years before who wanted nothing but an early death.

The queen needed all her strength now, for the government of Lord Salisbury suffered a fatal setback in the general election of 1892. The Liberals had only four more members than the Conservatives, and Liberal Unionists (anti-Home Rule) would support the Conservatives. But Gladstone could count on the votes of some eighty Irish members, and that was enough to give him control of the House of Commons.

Though Gladstone's eyesight was no better than the queen's, and his hearing decidedly worse, the Grand Old Man surged back into power at the age of eighty-two looking more than ever like some ancient Hebrew prophet proclaiming the wrath of God. Yet his mental vigor was undiminished and his oratory was as powerful as ever. However, this was his last chance to solve the Irish problem and he knew it.

The queen could not avoid inviting him to be prime minister, but she showed that the power of the sovereign had not altogether vanished by insisting, successfully, that one man whom she disliked (Sir Charles Dilke) should not become a member of the cabinet, and by persuading Lord Rosebery, against his own wishes, to accept the post of foreign secretary. When Mr. Gladstone arrived to receive his appointment, Victoria thought him "greatly altered and changed . . . his face shrunk, deadly pale with a weird look in his eyes, a feeble expression about the mouth, and the voice altered." Victoria was always inclined to make the worst of poor Gladstone's appearance, while the good Lord Salisbury always looked to her in the best of health and much younger than his years.

Gladstone, in fact, was fitter than the queen imagined. One afternoon while he was taking a quiet country stroll, he was charged by a cow that had gone berserk. Hurled to the ground, the quick-thinking prime minister "played dead" until the cow's attention wandered, whereupon he leapt up and dodged behind a tree. The cow was generally supposed to be an opponent of Home Rule.

Neither mad cows nor the gibes of his opponents diverted Gladstone from his course. The second Home Rule bill was introduced and the debate on its provisions lasted all summer. Tension was acute, and during a meeting of the committee of the House of Commons, more than insults were exchanged. In an angry speech, Joseph Chamberlain, once a supporter and now an opponent of Gladstone, compared him with Herod. An Irish member hurled back the obvious response: "Judas!" and in a moment distinguished members of the mother of Parliaments were brawling on the floor of the House of Commons. The Speaker, not present at committee meetings, was hastily summoned and order was restored.

Thanks to Gladstone's titanic efforts and the impressive loyalty he still commanded, the Home Rule bill was finally passed by the House of Commons. In the Lords, however, it was defeated by a large majority. By this time, the emotional force of the Home Rule argument was spent. Gladstone could not threaten the Lords (the usual tactics when the government was thwarted by the upper house—as in the 1884 reform bill) because there was no solid public support for Home Rule. Many of his own followers were secretly glad that the bill was dead.

The end of Home Rule foreshadowed the end of Gladstone's political career. The Grand Old Man, always inclined to be dogmatic about his own opinions, soon found himself in a head-on clash with his colleagues in the cabinet.

During the 1890's, international relations in Europe became extremely sensitive, with each nation hastily building up reserves of armaments. The Royal Navy, upon which the very existence of the empire depended, was old-fashioned, and a disastrous collision in the Mediterranean had robbed it of its best battleship. Conservatives and Liberals both agreed that the navy required a massive buildup. The prime minister, however, disagreed. At his age it was not surprising that he failed to recognize every new international trend.

IMPERIALISM

The uproar over the navy he described as scaremongering, and he adamantly refused to give in to the combined pressure of his entire cabinet. It was not a great moment to close a political career that had lasted sixty-two years, but not even Gladstone could continue in office under such circumstances. On March 1, he announced his resignation to his colleagues. It was a moving scene, and when it ended, the only eyes that remained dry were those of the Grand Old Man himself. That same day he made his last speech in the House of Commons—characteristically, a blistering attack on the Lords. Then he went to Windsor to take leave of the queen.

For the rest of his life Gladstone was tormented by the remembrance of Queen Victoria's coolness to him when he went to hand her his resignation. He felt that she had no feeling for him whatever, and he deeply resented her failure to say a word of thanks for all he had done for the country. To his son he said that the queen's mind had been poisoned against him by evil gossip, but this was not true. Nor was it true that the queen had no feelings at all about him; on the contrary, she loathed him intensely. With the gallantry that Gladstone always showed toward the crown in his stiff, formal way, he gave instructions that after his death his family should be "most careful to keep in the background all information respecting the personal relations of the queen and myself. . . ."

The truth of the matter was that relations between

the queen and her greatest prime minister had been so bad for so long that there could be no human contact between them. Victoria could be as relentless in her private feelings as Gladstone was in his public policy. And, like Gladstone himself, who became physically ill when he had to deliver a eulogy on his opponent Disraeli, the queen could not be insincere. She could not express gratitude that she did not feel.

Nevertheless, it is hard to excuse her cold-blooded dismissal of the prophet of English liberalism at the end of his illustrious career. One's sympathies must lie with the proud old statesman, bitter and heavy-hearted, as he took leave of that small, stiff figure sitting upright and impassive on a straight-backed chair.

The Liberal government continued for another year under the leadership of Lord Rosebery, whom Victoria liked, but in June, 1895, Lord Salisbury became prime minister at the head of a government supported by Conservatives and Liberal Unionists. It was a government that was to last longer than the queen.

The true period of European imperialism was very short. It reached its climax in the 1880's and 1890's in a succession of events often described as the "scramble" for Africa. In a few years the whole of that continent was divided among the major countries of Europe, with Britain coming out perhaps the best. There is no need to investigate these events closely in a life of Queen Victoria, but it is important to understand the spirit of the times, of which Victoria was a symbol and a representative.

The final twenty years of the nineteenth century were a period of growing national rivalries in Europe. One reason for this was the formidable new German Empire, which had upset the traditional balance of power. Another reason was the quickening pace of industrialization, with the ensuing race for new markets and new sources of raw materials. The partition of Africa was carried out in a peaceful, though sometimes dramatic, fashion, thus: If France takes this part, Germany can have that, and Britain this. Such compromises were worked out by men who often had very little knowledge of the actual territory they were dividing up.

New colonies in Africa were often acquired solely in order to prevent them from coming under the control of a rival European state. Gladstone refused to make Uganda a British protectorate in the face of vociferous warnings that if he did not, the Germans would take it. After his retirement, the British protectorate of that country was declared by Lord Rosebery.

Even at the climax of imperialism, governments were usually reluctant to take on new territorial responsibilities. Of course there were exceptions, and the chief exception in Britain was Joseph Chamberlain, a former Radical who split with Gladstone over

Home Rule and became secretary for the colonies under Lord Salisbury.

The feelings of the people were rather different. True Gladstonian Liberals opposed most imperialistic ventures, but the mass of the population were intoxicated with the idea of empire. This was not merely a greed for conquest and material gain: The Victorians believed they had a moral obligation to bring the benefits of British institutions and British culture to the deprived inhabitants of less fortunate lands. Cecil Rhodes, that dedicated imperialist, was not being altogether cynical when he described his activities as "philanthropy plus five per cent." The Victorians seldom questioned the rightness of what they were doing. The attitude of the many religious missionaries, who went into the "Dark Continent" to spread enlightenment and Christianity, was characteristic of the general feeling. Utterly confident of their own righteousness, the missionaries sang this hymn:

>From Greenland's icy mountains,
>From India's coral strand,
>Where Afric's sunny fountains
>Roll down their golden sand;
>From many an ancient river,
>From many a palmy plain,
>They call us to deliver
>Their land from error's chain.

The call for deliverance of course originated in the heads of those who sang the hymn.

It has been seen earlier how the British became involved in Egypt and found themselves unable to get out again. Their presence there irritated the French who, by virtue of their control of Algeria and Tunisia, were the dominant European power in North Africa. To compensate for the British presence in Egypt, the French decided to assert themselves in West Africa. Up to 1880 European settlements in this region hardly extended beyond a few coastal towns, but the sudden French activity around the Niger River prompted the British to declare a protectorate over the area. At a European conference held in 1884, the British kept the Niger region and the French took the area around Brazzaville, to the south, while Belgian rule was simultaneously acknowledged in the Congo.

Both the British and the French inevitably clashed with the peoples living in the interior of West Africa, and the resulting wars led to further expansion of the European areas. At length the British and the French came face-to-face at Fashoda on the Upper Nile in 1898. It was a tense moment for Europe, but war was avoided when the French withdrew, leaving the Upper Nile region to Britain. "An immense relief," the queen commented.

In East Africa, Germany was the main rival. After intense diplomatic activity a compromise was reached and Britain took the northern part (the present-day countries of Kenya, Uganda, and Tanzania) while Germany took the southern part (German East Africa). The British could afford to be more high-handed with the Portuguese, who were confined to Mozambique, and the Italians were checked when they were decisively defeated by Ethiopia, which was the one national state in Africa that preserved its independence throughout the colonial era (besides the tiny U.S.-supported Republic of Liberia).

The expansion of Britain in southern Africa was less obviously the result of European competition. There, the opponents of British rule were the nationalistic Boers. To prevent the Boers in the Transvaal from joining up with German South-West Africa, the British annexed Botswana in 1885. The following year gold was discovered in the Transvaal, and this changed the situation drastically.

The Boers, still basically a farming people, were rapidly outnumbered in the Transvaal by *Uitlanders* ("foreigners"), attracted by the economic boom. The unwanted Uitlanders were heavily taxed by the Boer government but enjoyed no civil rights. Their resentment built up.

Meanwhile, the prospect of more discoveries of gold galvanized Cecil Rhodes into action. The son of an English clergyman, Rhodes had come out to South Africa for his health, made a fortune out of diamonds, and entered politics in the British Cape Colony. He was partly responsible for the annexation of Botswana, and his ambition was to extend British territory the whole length of Africa, from Cape Town to Cairo.

In 1889 Rhodes founded the South Africa Company to search for gold and diamonds in central southern Africa: he hoped to find deposits as rich as those in the Transvaal. Within two years, vast new territories (Rhodesia, Zambia, and Malawi) were brought under British control. As Rhodes roared into Central Africa, the British government hung nervously to his coattails, approving his actions, after he had committed them, because it had very little choice.

Unfortunately for Rhodes and his associates, the mineral resources of the new territories proved disappointing. The rich gold mines of the Transvaal were not duplicated beyond its borders. Rhodes, who became prime minister of the Cape Colony in 1890, cast envious eyes upon the Transvaal. Not only did it possess the greatest riches, but its independent existence spoiled his plans for a great federation of the South African territories within the British Empire.

In the Transvaal itself, there was a rumor of rebellion among the Uitlanders. In December, 1895, a band of colonial police from Rhodesia, under the leadership of Dr. Leander Starr Jameson, crossed the Transvaal border and advanced on Johannesburg. Jameson, whose official title was Administrator of Rhodesia, expected a rising of the Uitlanders to coincide with his raid. But the rising never took place, and

Jameson and his men were quickly rounded up by the Boers. It then transpired that the raid had been planned by Rhodes himself—the prime minister of a supposedly friendly neighbor. (Joseph Chamberlain, the British colonial secretary, was also implicated, but this was not discovered for many years.)

"This affair is very unfortunate," the queen recorded with notable understatement. She was much more angry when she heard that her grandson, the German emperor, had sent a telegram to the president of the Transvaal, congratulating him on defeating the British raiders.

The Jameson Raid, which brought Rhodes's meteoric career to an end, deepened the hostility between Boers and British throughout southern Africa and led directly to the outbreak of the South African, or Boer, War, in 1899.

In the 1890's, English enthusiasm for the British Empire reached its climax, and imperial glory was the theme of the ceremonies celebrating the sixtieth anniversary of Queen Victoria's accession—the Diamond Jubilee. This time the kings and queens of Europe were not present (the German emperor wanted to come, but the queen thought he had better stay at home). Instead, the guests of honor were the representatives of the empire: prime ministers of the Dominions and colonies; Indian princes; African chiefs; Chinese from Hong Kong; and dignitaries from

Pacific islands that had not been mentioned in the geography books that Victoria studied as a girl.

Wearing an Indian-made dress and seated in a wheelchair ("as I cannot stand long"), the queen greeted them all with her usual perfect composure.

A brand-new train carried her from Windsor to London, the royal standard flying from the locomotive. There was no thanksgiving service in Westminster Abbey, as it would have been too tiring, and besides, the queen could not get up the steps. It was "queen's weather" again; after a misty start a brilliant sun burst through just as the queen touched a button that telegraphed her jubilee message throughout the empire: "From my heart I thank my beloved people, May God bless them!"

Victoria recorded her impressions: "A never-to-be-forgotten day. No one ever, I believe, has met with such an ovation as was given to me, passing through those six miles of streets. . . . The crowds were quite indescribable, and their enthusiasm truly marvellous and deeply touching. The cheering was quite deafening, and every face seemed to be filled with real joy. I was much moved and gratified." The accounts of other spectators show that the queen did not exaggerate the enthusiasm.

Her enjoyment of the celebrations was slightly marred by her fear for the safety of the densely packed people. For weeks she had been bombarding the home secretary with messages to make sure every precaution was taken against balconies collapsing or children being crushed.

Even die-hard republicans had to admit that if they *had* to have a monarchy, there could be far worse monarchs than Queen Victoria.

CHAPTER XVI

End of an Age

The Diamond Jubilee did not fill everyone with enthusiasm. The cause of republicanism in England still had its supporters, and even among the leaders of society, a sour note could sometimes be heard among the hubbub of applause. The aged Gladstone thought it was time Victoria gave up the throne to her son. The Prince of Wales had been heir apparent for fifty-five years and was now an elderly man himself.

Gladstone did not live to witness the end of the reign in which he had played so great a part. The Grand Old Man died at his country home on May 19 (Ascension Day), 1898. The queen could not bring herself to make a public statement of regret, but she sent a long and kindly telegram to Mrs. Gladstone on the day of the funeral. She was rather annoyed when she heard that the Prince of Wales had helped carry the coffin, and she asked him on what precedent and by whose advice he had done such a thing. With noble simplicity, the prince replied that he had looked for no precedent and asked for no advice.

Death was the great enemy in Victoria's last years. Her eldest daughter, the German empress, with whom she had corresponded every few days for forty years, contracted cancer in 1898 (she died in 1901, outliving her mother by a few weeks). Her second son, Prince Alfred, who had succeeded his uncle as duke of Saxe-Coburg-Gotha, died after a long illness in 1900. There were other deaths, too: several grandchildren, including Prince Alfred's eldest son; also, the beloved Lady Jane Churchill, a close friend of the queen for almost half a century.

At the age of eighty, the indomitable Victoria decided to visit Ireland. Nearly forty years had passed since her last visit and, characteristically, she hoped to bring to that country the peace and contentment that the politicians had failed to provide in the conflicts of the previous half century. The Irish sang "God Save the Queen," cheered loudly, and waved flags. Or some of them did. Victoria was too blind to see the angry faces scattered among the crowd, and too deaf to hear the occasional boo among the cheers. That there were no ugly incidents or demonstrations was partly the result of good security arrangements; but the vast prestige of the queen was enough to undermine the hostility of all but the fiercest nationalists. She moved about Dublin in a jaunty little cart drawn by a white donkey, and she wore a bonnet decorated with shamrocks. "Sure, you're a nice old lady," shouted one youthful Dubliner. After three weeks in Ireland, the queen departed on the royal yacht, the *Victoria and Albert*, with the cheers still ringing in her ears. She was quite sorry the visit had come to an end, but she confessed she was very tired and longed for "rest and quiet."

Victoria seemed to be always tired nowadays. Soon after her return from Ireland she wrote to a cabinet minister who had expressed the wish to retire from public life: "The Queen . . . feels that he is fully justified in wishing for rest. She wishes she could have the same . . . for she does need it."

She could easily have had it by resigning the throne to the Prince of Wales. Yet the thought hardly crossed her mind. Victoria may have wanted "rest and quiet," but she also enjoyed being queen.

Peace was a distant prospect in her last years. The Boer War, which began in October, 1899, and did not end until after her death, started badly for Britain. The tough, sharpshooting Boers adopted a form of warfare alien to the British regular army troops, and though outnumbered, they registered a succession of victories. But they could not hold out forever against the forces of the whole British Empire, and early in

1900 the tide began to turn. The last Boer army was defeated in September, but the Boers' skill in guerrilla fighting kept the war going another eighteen months.

The queen responded to the war with the same energy and optimism that she had shown during the Crimean War, forty-five years before. Sternly suppressing illness and fatigue, she hurried about, visiting hospitals and inspecting troops. Her old hands could still keep her knitting needles rattling, but she was annoyed when she discovered that the garments she had made had been given to officers, not to men in the ranks. As compensation, she sent out cans of chocolates to all the ordinary soldiers. One of these cans, carried in a breast pocket, saved a man's life when it stopped a bullet heading for his heart.

The early reverses suffered by their soldiers shocked the British public. The queen hastened to boost public morale. One pessimistic minister received a trumpet blast: "Please understand that there is no one depressed in this house; we are not interested in the possibilities of defeat; they do not exist."

During Britain's darkest days in World War II, this rousing message was engraved on millions of cards and hung in offices and homes throughout the country.

In the early years of her reign, the queen had often been attacked or satirized in the newspapers. Some of the cartoons that appeared in magazines like *Punch* were cruelly mocking, and even that great organ of British opinion, the *Times* of London, had sometimes blasted the royal court with heavy scorn. By the 1890's, such behavior was unthinkable. When the queen was trying to improve relations with Germany, she passed a message to the editors of the major English daily papers asking them to be more moderate about the German emperor and his people. Her wishes were carried out as if it was a perfectly ordinary thing for the queen to dictate editorial policy to the national press.

This was just one example of the informal power that the queen could exercise. Her executive power was slight (though not so slight as people assumed), but her huge and almost mystical prestige made it very difficult for anyone to act against her known wishes. To the people of Britain she had become more than a queen, more than an empress: it was hard to imagine England without her, for her very name seemed to stand for all that England meant. She personified her age and nation in a way that only her great predecessor Elizabeth had done.

At the same time, this magnificent figure was also a stout little old lady with rheumatism and bad eyesight who worried about cruelty to dogs and liked to gossip about the lives of servants.

On May 24, 1900, six extra mail sorters were hired at Balmoral to deal with a flood of four thousand telegrams. It was the queen's eighty-first birthday.

Victoria is shown here in old age with her son (later Edward VII), grandson (George V, right), and great-grandson (who, as Edward VIII, abdicated after a brief reign). (The Bettmann Archive)

"Again my old birthday returns, my 81st! God has been very merciful and supported me, but my trials and anxieties have been manifold, and I feel tired...."

Throughout the year the queen remained in close touch with events all over the world. Messages poured in from the British generals in South Africa; the prime minister was badgered with royal inquiries about a rebellion in China that resulted in the massacre of Europeans; the viceroy of India was called upon to explain why there were not more native Indians in the list of those recommended for honors.

Random extracts from the vast correspondence that arrived on the queen's desk during one month of the summer of 1900 give some idea of the range of her activities:

From her private secretary: "In consequence of your Majesty's representations 5,818 feather pillows were at once issued to the Cape hospitals and 1,450 to those at home."

From the emperor of Korea: "I beg to express to your Majesty my sincerest participation in the anxiety you must feel for the safety of your representative in Pekin..."

From General Lord Kitchener in South Africa: "Your Majesty will have heard by telegram the details of our recent march here. The troops are all well..."

From the empress of Ethiopia: "I received the little dog your Majesty sent me. He was a very nice little dog, but death took him from me."

During all this activity, Victoria was suffering with pain in her back that often prevented her from sleeping. She was persuaded to rest in the afternoons, though she deplored the loss of time. She managed to travel about London in a new, low carriage that was easy to get into, and also gave the crowds a better view. People noticed that she was wearing eyeglasses in public for the first time.

The hot summer of 1900 turned into a damp and gloomy fall. It was the weather, courtiers said, that made the queen feel ill. But courtiers, as she knew well, are flatterers. In December, she made her last public appearance at an exhibition of Irish industries in Windsor. Soon afterward she left the castle for her winter home at Osborne. The year ended in storms that set the English Channel churning angrily and shook the bare trees in Albert's garden at Osborne.

The queen could not sleep at night and dozed most of the day. In the evenings she roused herself to sign papers and dictate letters for a little while. But on January 14, her journal, uninterrupted for sixty-nine years, came to a stop. On January 15 she issued her last public order—a robust command to her ambassador in Berlin to refuse the offer of an honor from the German government.

On the eighteenth, her children were summoned, and a cautious public announcement was made: "The Queen has not lately been in her usual health . . ."

Europe paused. Inquiry, regret, hope, were registered in every capital in the world. President Kruger of the Transvaal, her opponent in war, gallantly expressed his wish that she might make a rapid recovery. The *Times* hoped that her vitality would see her through the crisis. But she became steadily weaker. The German emperor quietly joined the family at the queen's bedside. A public bulletin admitted she was "sinking."

As she slipped slowly away from her grieving family, it was the emperor William who, with his one good arm, supported her on the pillows, unmoving for two and a half hours. At 6:30 P.M., on January 22, 1901, Queen Victoria died. It was the end of an age.

The wind dropped and in a dead calm the royal yacht steamed from the Isle of Wight to the mainland, carrying the coffin in which Queen Victoria lay, her wedding veil covering her face. An endless line of ships fired their guns in a last salute. The coffin was white, draped with crimson, for Victoria had always hated funeral black. She agreed with Lord Tennyson that white was the best color for funerals.

A train with blinds drawn carried the coffin to London; people knelt down in the fields as it passed. A gun carriage waited to take the coffin to Windsor, and when the horses shied away, a detachment of sailors hastily filed between the shafts and dragged the carriage on foot. For a day or two the queen lay in state in the Albert Memorial Chapel, before the last stage of her journey to the mausoleum where a place had been waiting for her since the death of Albert, nearly forty years before. The family alone were present at the end, and as they left, snow began to fall and covered everything with white. For the last time, it was "queen's weather."

Throughout England and the British Empire, the death of Queen Victoria was received with shock, sadness, and even fear. She had been an old lady and her death cannot have been unexpected. Yet the public distress was deep and real. While she had been queen—and nobody could remember a time when she had not been—she was a reassuring sign of security and continuity. Her death, so soon after the beginning of a new century, seemed to signal a sharp break with the past. People felt that a new age was beginning, an age in which many things that had appeared solid and reliable in Victorian England would vanish forever. They looked forward to a future which promised many changes, and for a moment the self-confidence of the British people was shaken.

Three generations later, one can see clearly what the people of that time only dimly perceived. Already in 1901 the lines were being drawn in Europe for the carnage of World War I, which was to destroy the old Europe. Already the dogmas of Victorian England were being questioned (was the British Empire really so glorious?) and Victorian society was under attack. In literature and the arts, in architecture and design, Victorian ideas were being discarded. In industry and technology Britain, once supreme, had been overhauled by Germany, while developments in North America were making the European Industrial Revolution look tame and unenterprising. And in England, as in Europe, the voice of the masses was becoming steadily louder and more insistent.

The rapid changes that have occurred everywhere since Victoria's death have been even greater than the changes during her reign. Yet in 1901 Great Britain had changed more drastically since 1837 than in any comparable period previously.

When Victoria came to the throne, railroads were a novelty. Before she died she was able to watch automobiles rumbling along the streets of London. Cheap postal services were first introduced early in the reign. By 1901 messages could be sent by telegram and telephone. Such great men of the early Victorian period as the Duke of Wellington or Lord Melbourne would have been astonished to read the ideas of Charles Darwin on evolution, or Karl Marx on communism, or Sigmund Freud on psychology.

Perhaps the most dramatic change within Britain was the growth of the towns. At the beginning of the reign most people lived in the country. When the census of 1851 was taken, town dwellers had just overtaken country dwellers. By 1901 there were 25 million people living in towns in England and Wales, and this number was half again as large as the total population in 1851.

Great Britain was not a popular country in 1901. The Boer War, still going on, had lost Britain many friends in Europe. The sheer bulk of the British Empire and the obvious success of the British in political and economic advances created jealousy, resentment, or disapproval. In the twentieth century the empire has been dismantled, and Britain—under the pressure of war and economic competition—has faded from the ranks of great powers. It is a small country, after all. Yet it does not seem silly that Britain is sometimes called "Great" even today. Its unique achievements of the last century have not been forgotten. In science and literature, in industrial progress and imperial expansion, in political democracy and government reform, Britain set an example to the world—not always a good example, but certainly a striking one. Though often resented, the British achievement had to be—and still is—admired. Of that achievement, Queen Victoria was the living symbol.

Chronology

- 1819   Birth of Victoria (May 24).
- 1820   Death of King George III (grandfather).
Death of the Duke of Kent (father).
- 1830   Death of King George IV (uncle).
- 1832   Great Reform Act.
- 1837   Death of King William IV (uncle); Victoria becomes queen.
- 1839   Bedchamber Crisis.
- 1840   Marriage of Victoria and Prince Albert.
- 1841   Defeat of Lord Melbourne; Peel prime minister.
- 1846   Repeal of the Corn Laws; defeat of Peel.
- 1851   Napoleon III gains power in France.
The Great Exhibition.
- 1854   Outbreak of Crimean War.

VICTORIA: QUEEN AND EMPRESS

1855 Lord Palmerston prime minister.
1857 Indian Mutiny.
       Birth of Victoria's ninth and last child.
1858 Marriage of princess royal to future German emperor.
1861 Deaths of the Duchess of Kent (mother) and Prince Albert.
1864 John Brown becomes Victoria's personal servant.
1865 Death of King Leopold of the Belgians (uncle). Austro-Prussian War.
1867 British North America Act.
       Reform Act.
1868 Publication of *Leaves from the Journal of Our Life in the Highlands*.
       Gladstone prime minister (until 1874).
1870 Franco-Prussian War.
1872 Settlement of *Alabama* claims.
1874 Disraeli prime minister (until 1880).
1875 British purchase of Suez Canal shares.
1876 Victoria becomes "Empress of India."
1878 Congress of Berlin.
1879 Zulu and Afghan wars.
1880 Gladstone prime minister (until 1886).
1884 Reform Act.
1885 Death of General Gordon in Khartoum.
1886 Gladstone supports Home Rule for Ireland; Lord Salisbury prime minister (until 1892).
1887 Golden Jubilee.

1894 Retirement of Gladstone.
1895 Lord Salisbury prime minister.
     Jameson Raid.
1899 Outbreak of South African (Boer) War.
1901 Death of Victoria (January 22).

Note on Sources and Books

Most of the quotations in this book are taken from the following:

Letters of Queen Victoria, 1st Series, edited by A. C. Benson and Viscount Esher, 3 vols., 1908; *2nd Series,* edited by G. E. Buckle, 3 vols., 1926; *3rd Series,* edited by G. E. Buckle, 3 vols., 1932; all published by John Murray, London.

Further Letters of Queen Victoria, edited by Hector Bolitho, Thornton Butterworth, London, 1938.

Dearest Child: Letters of Queen Victoria and the Princess Royal, edited by Roger Fulford, Evans, London, 1963.

Some extracts from the queen's journal, not published elsewhere, have been taken from the standard modern biography of Queen Victoria by Elizabeth Longford, published in New York by Harper, 1965 (and available in a paperback edition).

Of the huge quantity of books about Victoria and her times, the following biographies are especially useful: Robert Blake (on Disraeli), Hector Bolitho (on Victoria), Lord David Cecil (on Melbourne), Roger Fulford (on the prince consort), and Sir Philip Magnus (on Gladstone).

The first modern biography of Queen Victoria, by Lytton Strachey, published in 1921, is a work of true literary genius though sometimes unreliable.

Index

Adams, Charles Francis, 141
Afghanistan, 165, 177, 178
Africa, 144, 202-208
Alabama claims, 141
Albert, Prince, 8, 13-14, 39-50, 51-52, 56, 58-59, 68, 75, 76, 86-87, 91-98, 170
   death, 97-98, 99-100
   education, 40
   illness, 92-97
   memorials, 103
   personality, 40-41
   plans exposition, 69-72
Albert Hall, 103
Alexander of Denmark, 103
Alexandria, 179
Alfred, Prince, 212
Alice, Princess, 102, 173
Alice in Wonderland, 121
Alsace, 138
Anesthetics, 46, 85

Assassination attempts, 47-48, 82, 114, 140
Augustenburg, 104
Australia, 144, 145, 146
Austria, 66, 73, 83, 109
Austro-Prussian War, 109

Bagehot, Walter, 19, 43
Balmoral Castle, 58, 111, 120, 170, 171
Beaconsfield, Lord. *see* Disrael
Beatrice, Princess, 87, 102, 108, 172
"Bedchamber Crisis," 36-39
Belgium, 205
Bell, Alexander Graham, 171
"Bertie." *See* Prince of Wales
Bismarck, Otto von, 104, 105, 109, 138, 195
Boers, 146, 147, 164, 177, 206, 208
   See also Boer War

INDEX

Boer War, 208, 213-214, 222
Bright, John, 109
Brighton Pavilion, 55-56
British East India Company, 168
British Empire, 143-153, 204, 222
British North America Act of 1867, 146
Brown, John, 111-115, 140, 173
Browning, Robert, 120
Buckingham Palace, 20, 27, 47, 55, 106-107
Bulgaria, 161, 163
Bulgarian Horrors and the Question of the East, The, 162

Cairo, 179
Cambridge, 94
Canada, 144, 145-146
Canada Act of 1840, 145
Canning, Lord, 150
Cape of Good Hope Colony, 146, 147. See also South Africa
Carlyle, Thomas, 18, 120
Carroll, Lewis. See Dodgson, C. L.
Caste system, 149
Cavendish, Frederick, 174
Chamberlain, Joseph, 174, 176, 199, 203-204, 208
Charlotte, Princess, 4
Chartism, 55
Christianity, 204
Churchill, Lady Jane, 212
Churchill, Randolph, 174, 187
Church of England, 133, 134, 158
Civil War, U.S., 95, 141
Clarendon, Lord, 67, 102
Clark, Sir James, 96
Colonies, 143-149, 164. See also British Empire
Congo, 205

Congress of Berlin, 163, 164, 178
Conroy, John, 6, 7, 9, 11, 12, 14, 17, 29, 30, 31
Conservative party, 36, 52-53, 63, 64, 115, 125, 127, 142, 156, 174, 184, 185, 198
Constantinople, 74, 75, 162, 163
Constitution, 24
Corn Laws, 51, 63, 64, 187
Crimean War, 77-81
  beginnings, 74-75
  See also Eastern Question
Crown. See Monarchy
Crystal Palace, 71, 72
Cyprus, 178

"Dark Continent." See Africa
Denmark, 104-105
Diary, Victoria's. See Journal.
Dickens, Charles, 120
Dilke, Sir Charles, 139, 140, 174, 198
Disestablishmentarianism, 134, 135
Disraeli, Benjamin, 63, 64, 100, 115-119, 121, 125, 127, 128, 129, 130, 133, 134, 142, 150-151, 155-166, 167, 170
  death of, 173
Dissenters, 133
"Dizzy." See Disraeli
Dodgson, C. L., 121
Dominions, 144, 147
  See also Australia, Canada, New Zealand.
Durham, Lord, 145

Eastern Question, 73-74, 81, 83
Edward VII. See Prince of Wales
Egypt, 157, 178-180, 205,

INDEX

Empire. *See* British Empire
"Ems telegram," 138
Ethiopia, 206
Eton, 190
Eugénie, Empress, 81

Faery Queene, The, 118
Famine, 55, 63
Fashoda, 205
Fenianism, 134, 138
France, 81, 82, 83, 138-139, 140, 163
Franco-Prussian War, 138-139, 140, 205
Frederick III, 87-88
Froude, J. A., 120

George I, 17
George II, 17
George III, 3, 17, 20
George IV, 4, 7, 17
Germany, 138, 140, 203, 205, 221
  See also Prussia
Gilbert and Sullivan, 128
Gladstone, William E., 19, 52, 64, 83, 118, 125, 128-137, 141-142, 155-156, 161-162, 166-167, 173-184, 185-187, 198-202
  death of, 211-212
"God Save the Queen," 190-191
Gordon, Charles George, 180-184
Grant, U. S., 171-172
Great Exhibition of 1851, 68-72

Hanover, king of, 60-61
Hastings, Lady Flora, 30-31
Helena, Princess, 102, 108
Hemophilia, 85-86
Hicks, Colonel, 180

High Church party, 158
Hinduism, 149-150
Home Rule, 174, 187, 188, 199, 200
Hospitals, 79
House of Commons, 33, 34, 63, 128, 186, 198, 200
Housing, 53
Hyde Park, 18-19, 71

India, 144, 147-154, 156, 159, 160, 162, 191
Indian Mutiny, 149-150
Industrial Revolution, 54, 68, 221
Iolanthe, 127
Ireland, 55, 63, 133, 134, 136-138, 173-174, 186-187, 212-213
Isandwhalla, 164, 165
Isle of Wight, 56
Italy, 66, 73, 206

Jameson, Leander Starr, 207-208
Journal, Victoria's 11, 21, 23-24, 31, 40, 60, 61, 97, 169, 176, 189, 198, 218

Kabul, 165
Karim, Abdul. *See* Munshi
Kensington Palace, 5, 7, 20
Kent, Duchess of, 4, 6, 13, 18, 20, 29, 31, 92
Kent, Duke of, 4-5
Khartoum, 181, 182, 183
Kipling, Rudyard, 143
Koh-i-Noor diamond, 72
Kruger, President, 219

Laborers. *See* Workers
Ladies of the bedchamber, 36
Leaves from the Journal of Our

231

INDEX

Life in the Highlands, 120, 121, 152, 173
Lehzen, Baroness, 7-8, 11, 12, 14, 15, 20, 45-46, 49-50
Leopold, King, 8, 11-12, 13, 20, 23, 39-40, 45, 107
Leopold, Prince, 85, 86, 173
Liberal party, 109, 127, 132, 141-142, 174, 184, 185, 198
Liberia, 206
Light Brigade, 78
Lincoln, Abraham, 108
Lords, House of, 200
Lorraine, 138
Louis Napoleon, 67
Louis Philippe, 60
Low Church party, 158
Lytton, Lord, 165

Mahdi, 180, 182, 183
Melbourne, Lord, 21-29, 30, 31, 33, 34, 37, 39, 45, 50, 51-52, 54, 55, 160, 169
Monarchy, in Britain, 17, 19-20, 100
  Victoria's views of, 19
Munshi, 193-194

Napoleon III, 81, 82
Navy, Royal, 200-201
Netherlands, The, 146
Newspapers, 76, 79, 114, 191, 215
New Zealand, 144, 146
Niger River, 205
Nightingale, Florence, 79-80

Osborne, 56, 155, 163, 218
Ottoman Empire, 73. *See also* Turkey

Palmerston, Lord, 64-68, 76, 79, 82-83, 104, 105, 106, 107, 129

"Pam."
  See Palmerston, Lord
Parliament, 4, 21, 33, 44, 69, 76, 101, 108, 115, 125, 135, 136, 137, 157, 159, 175
Peel, Robert, 34, 36-37, 52-53, 56, 63-65, 115, 132, 187
Plevna, 162
Population, 145
Portugal, 94, 206
Prince of Wales (Edward VII), 47, 61, 90-91, 94, 97, 102-103, 106, 113, 120, 137, 139-140, 151-152, 159, 211, 212, 213
Protestantism, 133
Prussia, 104-105, 109, 138
Public Worship Bill, 158
Punch, 214-215

Reform Act of 1832, 175
Reform Act of 1867, 119, 125, 175
Reform Act of 1884, 175
Religion, 133
Revolution, 55
Rhodes, Cecil, 204, 206-208
Roberts, General, 177
Rolle, Lord, 27
Roman Catholic Church, 133
Rosebery, Lord, 199, 202, 203
Rothschild, Lord, 157
Royal Titles Act of 1876, 159, 160
Russell, John, 67
Russia, 74-75, 81, 140, 162, 163, 165

Saint Paul's Cathedral, 140
Salisbury, Lord, 127, 158, 163, 175-176, 187-188, 198, 202

INDEX

Schleswig-Holstein, 104-106
Scotland, 138
   See also Balmoral Castle
Shelley, Percy Bysshe, 3
"Sick Man of Europe." *See* Turkey
Slums, 54
South Africa, 146-147, 164, 177
South Africa Company, 207
Spenser, Edmund, 118
Stanley, Lady Augusta, 138
Stockmar, Baron, 20, 43
Strachey, Lytton, 128
Sudan, 178, 180-181, 182
Suez Canal, 156-157, 158, 178-179

Tennyson, Alfred, Lord, 120
Thackeray, William, 72
Times of London, 106, 215, 219
   See also Newspapers
Towns, growth of, 221
Transvaal, 164, 177, 206, 207
Trent, 95
Turkey, 73-75, 161-163
Typhoid fever, 94, 96, 140

Uganda, 203
Uitlanders, 206, 207
United States, 95, 135, 141

Vicky, Princess, 47, 61, 87-90, 194-195, 212
   marries Frederick, 89
Victoria
   accession to throne, 15

on Americans, 172
as author, 120-121
birth, 5
and children, 49
coronation, 25, 27
death of, 219
Diamond Jubilee, 208-210
early education, 5-6
at eighty-one, 215-216
as Empress of India, 159-160
engagement, 43-44
and foreign policy, 66
Golden Jubilee
marriage, 45
at sixty, 170
ties to royalty, 103-104, 195-196
as widow, 99-102
Victoria and Albert, 213
Victoria of Battenberg, 196

War correspondents, 78
Wellington, Duke of, 31, 36, 71
West Africa, 205
Westminster Abbey, 25, 190
Whigs, 21, 34, 36, 37, 52, 64
William II, 90, 195, 219
William IV, 7, 9, 11, 12-13
   death of, 14, 17
Windsor Castle, 56, 167, 189, 192
Women and the vote, 175
Workers, 53, 54
World War I, 220

Zulus, 147, 164
   war with, 164-165